WRITING AN
INTERACTIVE
STORY

Pierre Lacombe, Gabriel Féraud, Clément Rivière

WRITING AN INTERACTIVE STORY

CRC Press
Taylor & Francis Group
Boca Raton London New York

CRC Press is an imprint of the
Taylor & Francis Group, an **informa** business

CRC Press
Taylor & Francis Group
6000 Broken Sound Parkway NW, Suite 300
Boca Raton, FL 33487-2742

CRC Press is an imprint of Taylor & Francis Group, an Informa business

No claim to original U.S. Government works

Printed and bound by CPI Group (UK) Ltd, Croydon, CR0 4YY on acid-free paper

International Standard Book Number-13: 978-0-367-41030-8 (Hardback)
International Standard Book Number-13: 978-0-367-41031-5 (Paperback)

Visit the Taylor & Francis Web site at
http://www.taylorandfrancis.com

and the CRC Press Web site at
http://www.crcpress.com

To my incredible sister Diane, the muse who has always inspired me, To my sweet parents Florence and Régis, authors of my life, in which they are the heroes, To Chloé, the fearless adventurer who accompanies and supports me

Pierre Lacombe

To my fiancée Charlie, my mother, my sister, her two wonderful children, to Platypus because he did well to freshen up, and to the whole Dussine family and Farquhar. And last but not least, Joëlle Sevilla and Bernard Belletante for their knowledge and support.

Clément Rivière

Pierre Lacombe

Gabriel Féraud

Clément Rivière

SUMMARY

PREFACE: THE INTERACTIVE ADVENTURE BEGINS*

Life is the most fantastic interactive story there is. We make choices every day, at any time. We are defined as individuals by the choices we make. That's the existentialist point of view from the philosopher Sartre, for example. We are all the result of our choices, and that's what I believe too.

Everything I attempt to do in interactive storytelling is to imitate life. And it's an immense challenge because life is so complex that all we can do in interactive storytelling is to reconstruct a very simplified version of existence. It's an immense, yet exciting challenge.

The way we tell stories hasn't really changed since Aristotle established the rules of dramaturgy around 2,500 years ago.

Interactive writing is, in my opinion, the first (or at least the biggest) revolution in our way of telling stories.

For about twenty years now, I have been fascinated by the fact that interactive storytelling is an art where the author creates with his audience. That's what makes interactive storytelling so unique and different from other forms of art.

It is interesting because by being active in the story, the player learns about himself. It's not about passively watching a film, but rather being an actor in the film: making choices and facing up to the consequences of them. This questions the player's moral values and who he really is. The experience acts as a sort of mirror for the player.

....

*From exclusive interviews.

I am convinced that it's a very demanding art. It's an art because you obviously have a need to be creative, you have to create emotion. It's technical because you need to learn certain essential things, and to learn them you need to see failure as a success. Both of them are important.

It is also a difficult are because there are not many projects or examples of this art – or at least not as many as I would like.

When we began working on *Fahrenheit* and *Heavy Rain*, in the video game industry we were looked at as if we were extraterrestrials. We would go see people to talk about interactive stories, and the people thought of adventure games with puzzles and riddles. Honestly, no one took us seriously.

The heavyweights releasing actions games would ask us: "Who needs storytelling?"

After *Heavy Rain*, we started seeing things change. Some people were working on some *First Person Shooters* told us. "We're big fans of *Heavy Rain*. How can we put some storytelling in our game?"

So, we saw storytelling appear a little bit everywhere, even in car and sports games!

Then, they started taking interest in emotion. At the time of *Fahrenheit*, when we would talk about emotion, everyone would retort: "Emotion? Who needs that in a video game?" But with *Fahrenheit*, and especially with *Heavy Rain*, the industry has learned that it's precisely emotion that enhances the experience and makes it more impactful. It's the emotion that leaves a trace in players' minds and makes your gaming experience something they'll remember for a long time.

When I started working twenty years ago, I had not point of reference. There were no games that did what I wanted to do. There were a few people doing interactive storytelling research, be it was still rather abstract. They would discuss the theory of things that really didn't exist – at least not as a *mainstream* product.

I ended up writing everything myself on my first project, *Nomad Soul*, without any idea about how it all worked. In twenty years, I've made just about all imaginable mistakes possible, which allow me to know what I'm doing today.

I've developed my own techniques, my own grammar, but it's all taken my twenty years.

I think having a point of reference like this book could be infinitely useful for both young and experienced authors alike and give them a twenty-year head start.

Nothing can replace experience and solving problems on your own because it's the best way to understand them, but, at the same time, if you can have a bit of experience of someone who's worked on the subject for years up your sleeve, that helps you save lots and lots of time.

David Cage, BAFTA 2013 Best Story (Heavy Rain)[1]

BRITISH ACADEMY
GAMES AWARDS

---

1. The BAFTA (British Academy of Film and Television Arts) Games Awards is the most prestigious international awards ceremony in the profession for writing video game stories.

Let's lay the foundation.

With interactive scriptwriting, the spectator becomes an actor in the work. The player's choices have consequences, and the player creates his own experience. Thus, the player is experiences more emotion than a film or reading a book because he feels responsible.

The goal isn't to teach lessons. There is no happy or sad ending. The player makes his choices and must accept them. Like in real life. Just because he made a bad choice doesn't mean he's a bad person. This allows us to take an introspective look at ourselves To ask questions about who we are.

With interactive storytelling, we're able to convey and even stronger message because the player is the one who experiences his own choices and faces the consequences. Let us be very clear, it's the ultimate form of storytelling.

It's not about the future of storytelling because classic scriptwriting will always exist with films, series and classic games. However, it's a new means of storytelling that shows enormous promise, particularly in video games, where it has really taken off in the last ten years.

Story-based games are becoming more and more popular, and interactive storytelling a big bright future ahead of it.

And I know what I'm talking about.

At Dontnod, we didn't expect *Life Is Strange* to be so successful. Suddenly, we had a huge hit that exceeded the whole team's expectations. What really struck me were all the emails we received: thank-you emails, testimonials of love...

We managed to touch so many people. Obviously, the was also professional recognition, awards. But it's the recognition of the people that ultimately is the most important.

And the more awards the game won, the more it was recognized and had the chance to win more of them. And, in the end, we were nominated in five BAFTA categories. We won the BAFTA for Best Story. For me, as a scriptwriter, it was incredible. This award was all the more special because it resonated with the public's feedback.

In France, most people, even in the professional world, really don't know what a BAFTA award is and how valuable it is. The video game remains well recognized, even if it's in the process of changing.

With the success of *Life Is Strange*, I am very proud that we were able to show that it was possible. We set a new bar. And personally, I am very proud we were able to bring about change in the media I work in. I'm thrilled that it's inspiring and that it's becoming a calling because the world needs good stories. The more people write good stories that touch others, the more I think that it can change the world.

And a book, this book, can change things.

I dream that one day being a video game author will be as recognized as cinema is for the general public. If people see books that talk about interactive scriptwriting and read them, it's more likely they will change their point of view.

With this book, we're at the beginning of a great adventure!

Jean-Luc Cano, BAFTA 2015 Best Story (Life Is Strange)

BRITISH ACADEMY
GAMES AWARDS

FOREWORD

Your mission, reader, if you accept it, is to read and take away from this book whatever seems important to you and your storywriting.

If you already write stores, go to *Welcome, young Padawan!*

If you haven't written any stories yet, go to *Welcome, young Padawan!*

Afterward, or if you decide to not consult either of these sections, go to the*Introduction!*

WELCOME, COMRADE!

Are you an author? That means everything and nothing all at the same time, though we're actually talking about the perpetrator of a crime. If you are an author, we hope your only crime is a literary one... All joking aside, at one time, people talked of authors and playwrights, but then came along cinema with its specific needs and, over the last century, rarely have so many stories been produced in such a wide variety of ways. You are thus part of all these "content drivers," as we say nowadays in our even-connected world. Connections? Humans have always had them, particularly with stories. The stories get told, retold, internalized or shared.

There is nothing more volatile and more eternal than a good story.

But what about an interactive story? The number of authors working with this type of writing has fluctuated, even if one can say that it's an invention from the last century. An invention that was first book based, then incorporated into video games before invariably finding itself in one just as easily as the other. Simply put, for an interactive book, a publisher is required to point it out to the reader, whereas for a videogame, the interactivity, we hope for your sake, is obvious.

Either you already write interactive stories or you're interesting in this field. Be demanding with this book – whatever doesn't interest you, don't bother with it, but whatever bothers, titillates or surprises you, give it a second thought.

⌐ And now, go to part 1!

WELCOME, YOUNG PADAWAN!

Do you want to write? Take special note: even if you want to write a video game, which may not contain any text at all, you better write a story. You can start a game without a story, but if it's more than just a brick breaker, you're going to feel something is missing.

Let's not fool ourselves: if you've never written a story, you're starting with the most difficult task. Either you put this book down and write some other texts and pick it back up later, or you drawn on the one resource you'll have to push to its limit: your will.

Note that throughout this book, we have opted to use the term "female player" instead of "male player." It's not just about underscoring the importance of our audience, it's also about illustrating that games based on interactive stories are the standard-bearer of an ever-growing female audience, as demonstrated by several video game console/PC market studies and the success of mobile narrative-based games such as *Choices*, *Episodes* or *Is It Love?*[2].

....

2. Mobile interactive storytelling platforms with a credit-based business model, purchased in 2017-2018 for tens of millions of dollars by giants Nexon, Tencent and Ubisoft.

PART 1

INTERACTIVE STORYTELLING, A MULTIMEDIA ART

Interactivity in stories has existed since language was invented. By adapting your story to each person, you create a unique bond that helps open a door to your universe while allowing you to better understand your audience.

Today, interactive storytelling is used in*entertainment*, education and communications, in many different kinds of media, forming a new form of art.

1. WHAT IS AN INTERACTIVE SCENARIO?

An interactive scenario lets the reader choose how the the story he's reading unfolds. Consequently, a videogame scenario is by nature interactive because the player has the possibility, albeit minimal, to participate in how the game unfolds. The notion of interactivity will thus depend on the choices proposed, their quantity and their quality, as well as the endings proposed by the scenario, with the same constraint on quantity and quality.

The notion of play is essential in building an interactive scenario. Even if your interactive story takes on life in a book, we will be talking about a "player" and not a "reader."

An interactive scenario involves writing a story you play. And more precisely, the art of the interactive story consists of writing *stories* you play. The possible endings you propose, the more paths you will have proposed to reach them and, thus, more stories for your player.

So yes, the difficulty appears right away: you virtually have to write everything, envision everything. And you work yourself to death before you even finish.

Don't forget that, if interactivity is at the heart of the interactive scenario, it's a scenario: it's going to frame the universe, the characters, the adventures, everything that's going to interact with the player.

By way of comparison, a scenario for a game such as *Candy Crush* doesn't exist. There is no scenario. Your player can interact of course, but the universe, while very colorful, is very limited, just like all the possible interactions. This example may seem extreme, but it's a basic way to show that while every video game offers interactivity, like all games out there, it doesn't necessarily mean there is an interactive scenario behind it.

Video game specialists will explain that if you have to decide what effect an action, etc. produces, we would agree in saying that more than anything it's about elements of entertainment, *gameplay*, but it's not a story. Soccer has rules. A soccer game reproduces these rules and needs *gameplay* so you can enjoy playing it, at least one would hope, but there's no story, much less interactive storytelling. A tournament isn't enough.

Yet, nowadays, sports games are incorporating storytelling and offer players the possibility of creating a character who will have a brilliant career. The NBA 2K license is an example that is already a powerhouse in sports games Despites its shortcomings, the career, as proposed by Spike Lee in NBA 2K16, lets the player live the myth of the self-made man by climbing the ladder to glory (the NBA title) and further still by attaining the Grail (the equivalent of which is induction in the *Hall of Fame*). It's about sitting next to his majesty, Michael Jordan.

The player is thus transcended by her avatar. The character touches us deep within with her success because, deep down, everyone wants to live a wonderful story. For the experience to be complete, our character must become a legend. That's all!

Player rankings are found in sport simulations just as much as in story-based games. It's not about knowing whether I'm first, it's about comparing my experience. *What did I miss? Did I manage to explore everything? Am I the only one who made this choice?...*

One can imagine that, in the long term, sports games will shift toward story-based experiences and will, thus, be more and more interactive. The more a player feels her avatar is unique, the more complete her experience will be. And that's how sports games taken inspiration from roleplaying games...

If you play *World of Warcraft* online, you're playing a *massive multimedia online role playing game* (MMORPG), an online version of a roleplaying game. Virtually, in the strict sense of the term, you can do whatever you want, and even do nothing. If you want, there's no story, and you can stroll around the universe. Or you can meet other players and interact with them, not least by fighting against them. Or, and here's where you enter a multitude of interactive stories, you complete quests that the game designers propose to you. In a way, a MMORPG is an interactive universe that allows you to choose the interactive stories you want to play.

Between these two types of games, the *casual game* in the style of *Candy Crush* and the MMORPG in the style of *World of Warcraft*, you have a wide variety of possible interactive stories. To prevent getting lost giving advice that's too general, we will often make reference to the text-based interactive scenario. This is typically the kind of scenario where you'll have to write the most, and that's what this book is really interested in. If you write an interactive scenario for a text-based game, you'll have the ability to write for any kind of game requiring an interactive scenario.

Afterward, you'll first need to find the essential element without which nothing will be possible: the desire to write.

Let's assume you meet this prerequisite. To create your scenario, you need a story, or at least one subject. You'll understand, if you have no idea in mind, no topic, nothing at all, you attempt any methods in any order you want, and nothing will happen.

It's not about having your whole story in mind but rather having at least one element around which you can embroider, knit, unravel, in brief, build your interactive scenario.

To help you on your adventure, we went and got opinions and testimonials from writers recognized for their work in interactive storytelling.

Thus, you can read the point of view of:

- David Cage, writer and director of *Heavy Rain*, *Beyond: Two Souls* and *Detroit: Become Human*, at Quantic Dream.
- Jean-Luc Cano, writer of *Life Is Strange*, at Dontnod.
- Sybil Collas, narrative designer for *Vampyr*, at Dontnod.
- Benjamin Diebling, roleplaying game writer and videogame director (Quantic Dream).
- Erwan Le Breton, editorial narrative manager, at Ubisoft.
- FibreTigre, director of *Out There* and *Out There Chronicles* 1 and 2, at Mi-Clos.
- Joe Pinney, director of *The Wolf Among Us*, at Telltale Games.
- David Bowman, production director, at Telltale Games.
- Thomas Veauclin, director and art director of *The Council*, at Big Bad Wolf.

If you already a story to write in mind, got to *I have story!*
If you have some ideas but it's not all clear yet, go to *I have an idea!*
If you have a work order and, in particular, if you've gone blank, go to *I have an order!*

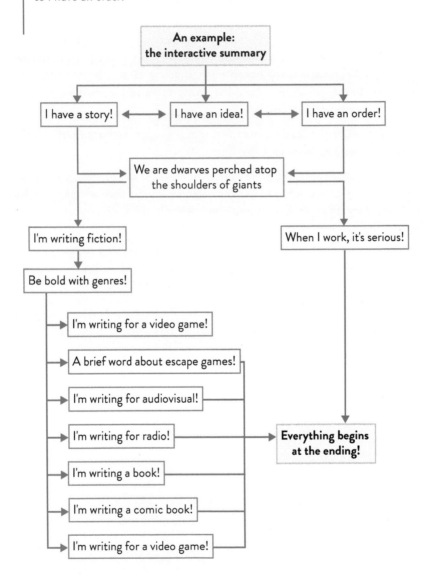

I HAVE A STORY!

This is the simplest situation for you, but there is absolutely no guarantee you'll be successful. In fact, you know what to write, you have an idea for a well developed story, you just need to use it to your advantage.

The first danger is discouragement. In fact, if you already have your whole story in mind, you may yearn to put the idea in writing, to give it shape. Just because you know, or you have the intuition, in addition to taking a lot of time while you work on it, your story may evolve considerably.

This is the second danger, rigidity. You have a story in mind, and there is nothing harder than abandoning a good idea mid-route. By building your scenario, you realize that this superb scene, as brilliant as it may be, in the end doesn't stick, it doesn't belong in this story. You'll try to put it in there anyway, but nothing doing. So, set it aside. If it's a good idea, you'll naturally put it in another story, where it will fit like a glove. And be smart, don't forget that you're writing an interactive scenario, so another branch could suit it quite well.

The third danger is the interactivity. Don't forget you're not writing a story for it to be read or seen, it's a story to be played, and an interactive scenario requires you to put the player in the driver's seat. You establish the possible routes, but the player has to be able to play, to discover your story through interaction, not as a spectator. Consequently, you really have to weigh your story. Will it stand up to interactive scenario cutting?

Later you'll see, there are many tools you can use to work on your story, to assess how feasible it is as an interactive scenario. In the following chapters, as you go you'll just have to see whether it fits with what's needed.

Go to *We are dwarves perched atop the shoulders of giants*, or, if you're curious, take a look at *I have an order!* and *I have an idea!*

I HAVE AN IDEA!

You have a nascent idea, or several, but you feel there's potential to create a story. A strong idea generally underpins stories and novels, and this is the approach you'll use to deploy your skill and imagination.

But is this necessary for writing an interactive scenario?

You can't give an idea a go when writing an interactive scenario. This is the best way to never finish it (the wisest solution) or, if you're tenacious, to make a bonsai. What do you mean, bonsai? You'll notice, we often talk about arborescence in interactive scriptwriting, and the more developed the arborescence is, the more choices the scenario offers to the player, the more immersive the experience is and the longer the game lasts. A bonsai, well, is an teeny-tiny tree trimmed by a gardener so that it remains a dwarf tree.

By starting an interactive scenario without any preparation, you'll might start to feel that your arborescence is getting too big and, not knowing where you want to go, logically you'll end up cutting back on everything and stunting your story in order to propose something viable and presentable. This is an exaggeration, but you get the idea. You wanted to write a novel, but since it's hard to see the end, you bottle it up in a short story, which will clearly not be satisfying.

This is because an idea alone is not a enough to form the basis for an interactive scenario: you *truly* need a solid story. Your player is going to be able to make choices and interact with her environment. If the basic idea is not fertile enough, when you work on your story, you'll soon drawing a blank.

So what do you do? You see the potential for any interactive story, but how can you be sure? It's a time-consuming task, but you're right to ask yourself the right questions before starting. As a strategy, you need a battle plan, which you'll adapt to your creative needs, and advance recognition. You'll define the goals to reach, and you'll soon understand that, for your, this means endings. The goal of an interactive scenario is not to have *one* ending but *many* endings; a little like how a strategy defines primary and secondary objectives, you will focus on primary and secondary endings. And it's by reflecting on those that you'll see whether your idea, or your set of ideas, are up to the task.

And why not tell your story to a friend or family member to get a first impression? Regardless of the feedback, don't forget that there is no wrong subject. It's our ability to build a narrative and our perseverance to rewrite it that counts. Moreover, avoid telling it xtimes. The desire to write it may run out soon after. Having a good subject is invaluable.

> Go to *We are dwarves perched atop the shoulders of giants*, or, if you're curious, take a look at *I have an order!* and *I have a story!*

I HAVE AN ORDER!

You have an interactive scenario to do. Something not uncommon in the writing profession, someone calls on you.

You've accept the project because you do need to making a living. You really don't care at all for the topic and don't know anything about it. Well, you're going to find out really quickly whether or not you're made for this profession.

Note that we're using this extreme example because if you accepted a work order for which you already have a strong story or some emerging ideas, you'll more likely be in the preceding situations. Let's be clear: there is nothing dishonorable or anti-artistic about a work order; the project idea, whether the universe, the characters, etc. just don't come directly from you. However, most of the time, getting into the project and tackling it won't pose a problem, even if you need to watch our for the project specifications.

Here, we're envisioning the worst, you're cornered.

You need to gather documentation. Which is always valuable in any case, but here, you are clearly blanking, so you need to tackle the problem head on. If it's a game universe you're indifferent about (car race?), play these games. If it's a topic or subject you've never worked with (cannibalism in a school setting?), gather information.

In your case, with whatever documentation you gather, you'll begin to nourish your imagination. And in this regard, you need to learn to gather documentation, too. Finding valuable documentation to work on a subject is not limited to doing a Google search.

That's all nice, but how does one get an order anyway? The production company is going to receive dozens of proposals for a contract. Try to relate the subject to your own experience. Transform the constraint, don't be vague, be precise in your presentation. Propose an alluring document that captivates your reader.

Make yourself indispensable by using things you've gained over your career. What makes me qualified to work on this order?

Tip: be attentive to the number of rewrites you might be asked to do. You should negotiate a limit, otherwise your client may try to make never-ending changes. Each rewrite should have a cost. Don't hesitate to consult the part of this book dedicated to selling an interactive scenario.

 Go to *We are dwarves perched atop the shoulders of giants*, or, if you're curious, take a look at *I have an idea!* and *I have a story!*

PRO INSIGHT

Jean-Luc, what would you like to tell about your experience in interactive storytelling?

Jean-Luc Cano: I really don't have a favorite subject. But unconsciously, once I have a story I like, I always relate to it better. I write about what makes me feel, and what I feel like writing about, because no one else will do it for me.

Do you have any stories in stock?

Oh of course, but I hardly write for myself anymore. People hire me. I need to get paid for what I write. There are tons of stories I'd like to write, but I won't write them unless I get hired. I have tons of ideas, but to write them, I need to sell them.

What advice can you give to authors who would like to start working in interactive storytelling?

They need to get familiar with the profession they're going to work in. You need to buy books to learn to write but also learn more by going to studios. The write well for media, you need to know it and know its codes. You also have to know how to work as a team and accept that your story goes through the grinder of *gameplay*, production, etc. You need to be prepared for the fact that your story is going to change and evolve. That's the hardest part.

Sybil, what meaning do you give to your interactive stories? Do you have favorite topics that appear in your stories?

Sybil Collas: I'm fond of family topics, the relationships between friends or communities, the subtleties inherent to family ties between individuals. Exploring human relationships is endless. I think video games are the best medium to explore them in. The interactivity and the impact on the player are the best way to let your audience share their own opinions and their own moral values on a subject that is much too vast for your own point of view to describe it alone.

The judgment of others, biases, and conventional attitudes are also other subjects I like to explore, but I have yet to build an entire game around these topics. These topics emphasize most of my work because they are natural derivatives of my values. More commonly, any author or writer puts a part of himself in his stories, whether consciously or not. This might be his values, clichés, big moral concepts or beliefs.

Joe, what sense do you give to your interactive stories?

Joe Pinney: I love stories of young people on a quest for meaning. When I work with other people's intellectual property, most of the time I'm looking for something that personally touches me or something I can honestly talk about. I like to pose to players the same questions I post to myself. If I feel tenderness about something, or a little fear, that's generally a good sign.

WE ARE DWARVES PERCHED ATOP THE SHOULDERS OF GIANTS

Whether you have a story, an idea or nothing at all, always remember to consider your subject in light of what has already been done. You can very well tell yourself that a sailor who kills creatures in a laboratory is a great idea, one you've never had before, but if you don't do any background research, you won't know whether you're the first person to have the idea, or one of many.

We don't create from nothing, and your ideas will mainly come from others, more precisely, from you culture. Whether its your general culture, cinematography, literature, video games, art, etc. There is nothing shameful or bad about it: cultural enrichment nourishes your imagination. You do need a minimum of originality. We hope you have the ultimate idea, but beware of originality for originality's sake. There are certain things human beings never do because they aren't interesting (breathing only through your left nostril) or because they're bound to fail (climbing Everest shirtless).

Your own stories, the ones you live and the ones you write, your personal experience, will also come to nourish you creative ability. In the long term, you will quickly have an intuition of what you can do when an idea comes your way or when the client talks to you about their project. Intuition is the ability to mobilize your knowledge, you skills and your experience to tackle a problem and find a solution for it. If we look at an engine, a mechanic knows when to use a size 12 wrench. And there's a good chance his intuition is right. And so for you, when someone asks you to create a story, you'll often have an idea of which direction to propose. And since you're a good professional, you'll then check to see if your intuition was right: you need your ego to complete your story, but you shouldn't let yourself be blinded by it.

We have already talked about strategy – writing an interactive scenario follows the same principle. You've defined your plan, but as you do your work your intuition will guide you on the right direction to take, what turning points to make, how to start the game, how to achieve the goals, the endings. A comparison to a strategist isn't as far off as you might think, since his enemy is his opponent's intelligence, his adversary's strategy, whereas for you, your adversary is the player. And while you don't know the player's abilities, desires or tastes, which is part of your uncertainty, you have the high ground: a well prepared scenario, which increases your chances of victory. This victory is strictly the player's enjoyment, no more no less. And to get a little closer to your goal, it's better to rely on your work rather than chance. For its part, you can always influence it with the game's mechanics.

Again, we insist one last time: an interactive scenario is something you play, something you live. It's not something you watch, no matter how clever you make it.

> If you are working on *serious game*, go to *When I work, it's serious!*
> If you're working on fiction, go to *I write fiction!*

David, do you have a method for avoiding a lack of inspiration?

David Cage: Over the years, I've developed several techniques for counter the fear of a blank page that all authors encounter. Many authors get paralyzed by the fear of a blank page and don't know where to start. This can be very worrying. So, I've developed a method that really works well for me: I write what I'm thinking in real time.

It's something rather strange that I wouldn't want any to read because most of what I write is probably stupid, but to summarize, I write everything that comes to mind as I'm reflecting. It's interesting because it's a true reflection of my creative process. Even if most of it is useless, there are occasionally some interesting things, and I can actually go back over my train of thought to understand how I got to a certain idea.

Sometimes, you get an idea and you think about something else, and you lose track of this great idea you had only moments ago. With this method, if I suddenly have a brilliant idea, I can easily go back to it and resume writing from that point.

This is what I call "*natural thinking*" or "*writing thinking*" and for me it's very effective. It also gives you a sense of always being busy. You're no longer worrying about the blank page because you're constantly writing, thinking. This creates a stimulating creative environment where you can really explore your train of thought because you make it happen.

What would you like to tell us, Jean-Luc?

Jean-Luc Cano: I basically always have the same problems. Once I start imagining a story, the first thing I ask myself is what I feel like learning as a truth about life at the end of the story. Personally, what touches me the most is adolescence. I think it's the most difficult period of life, but also the best. I'm also interested in basic universal questions: how to be happy? What happens after we die? The questions touch me, but they also touch everyone else. I'm a normal man who writes normal stories. I lay myself bare: That's the only true way to touch other others. With interactive storytelling, we're capable of conveying an even stronger message because the player is the one who experiences his own choices and who faces the consequences.

2. WHERE INTERACTIVE STORIES ARE USED

WHEN I WORK, IT'S SERIOUS!

So you have to write a *serious game*? This term has recently appeared with video games. We could oversimplify things by saying that *serious games* already existed in the form of board games, etc., but we'll just stick to *serious games* in video form. You know, learning games is nothing new. Learning video games, however, is a lot more recent in human history. The notion of learning is to be taken in a broad sense; this can vary from a player's reaction to a situation to hardcore immersive simulation training. With new technologies, the matter of training has become more critical than ever, and there is a lot of stuff to use from many *serious games*.

In this book, our purpose isn't to tackle *serious games*, but if there has to be interactivity between a player and a game, this is well within their domain.

Right now, if you're working on something other than a serious game, go to *I'm writing fiction!*, or dive into the heart of the subject and go to *Everything begins at the ending!*

I'M WRITING FICTION!

Whether you have a story or some ideas, with fiction, it's good to ask yourself about genres. Why? For the setting

We quite agree, a genre is a label you put on a book, film or game. More than anything, it's there to help us identify things, but without having the tools to classify and identify, it's much more complicated to know what we like. With a genre, we use a very valuable to guide how we build a story.

If take *Call of Duty*, for example, and it's not presented to me at least as an action game, I could be disappointed since I prefer management games on sustainable development.

Conversely, if a film is presented to me as *slasher* film and there isn't one victim after another, I'm going to be disappointed.

You see, for the player, viewer and reader, a genre has meaning. Few people want to see, read or buy something without having an idea of what it might be.

For a scriptwriter, the genre is both a constraint and an advantage. A constraint, because in theory you have to respect the rules of the genre. It's hard to imagine a shooting game with shooting, for example. And it's an advantage because it gives you a setting wherein you can develop your story and even adapt it. We know, for example, that searching for ammunition is an essential element of the *gameplay* ; as for the story, you really need to explain why one shoots at one character or another.

And the evolution has been very clear in the 21stcentury. With so many genres out there, there are more and more mixed genres. So, it's possible to use several codes. That said, at the start, it's undoubtedly better to be content to work in one genre for a story instead of mixing everything up – but if you're really feeling it, go for it!

Simply put, always remember that, in an interactive scenario, it's always more complicated. To put it one way, if you make a poor mix by borrowing certain branches in your story, your player might get thrown into the other genre unexpectedly. While surprise is a key element of suspense, the surprise has to be a good one. The player mustn't stop because the story suddenly no longer corresponds to what she was expecting. However, if she's excited to discover a new facet of the story, this is a success!

This is why we advise beginners to choose one genre and stick to it. However, videogame culture, like manga and anime, helps us in this regard. If you story fits a genre, you can offer a clearly more eccentric universe.

It's very important to distinguish between the universe of your story and the genre you wish to use for it. It's a matter of having the right formula, but rest assured, or take a deep breath, we're clearly going to address the matter of the universe in detail.

You want some genre examples?

- A film noir? Watch *Touchez pas au grisbi [Don't Touch the Loot]* by Jacques Becker.
- A cyberpunk novel? Read *Hardwired* by Walter John Williams.
- A war game? Play *Call of Duty*, released by Activision and many more.
- An adventure film? Watch *Raiders of the Lost Ark* by Steven Spielberg.
- A fantasy novel? Read *The Lord of the Rings* by J.R.R. Tolkien.
- A science fiction game? Play *Mass Effect*, developed by BioWare.

If you're writing a scenario for a roleplaying game, go to *I'm writing for a roleplaying game!*
If you're writing a scenario for audiovisual, go to *I'm writing for audiovisual!*
If you're writing a scenario for radio, go to *I'm writing for radio!*
If you're writing a book, go to *I'm writing a book!*
If you're writing a cartoon, go to *I'm writing a comic book!*
If you're writing a video game, go to *I'm writing for a video game!*
Obviously, you can very well write in more than one domain.
And if you're curious, read everything!

I'M WRITING FOR A ROLEPLAYING GAME!

It's a good idea to take a moment to talk about roleplaying games (RPGs). For many players of videogames, it's a term that refers to MMORPGs, not least because the much-talked-about *roleplaying game* is in the name. Video games started flirting with roleplaying games very quickly because if you play a character, as you do in the old yet mythical *Alone in the Dark*, you play a role. It's clear we've come a long way from the first *point-and-click* games, yet this doesn't mean, however, that these games are necessarily outdated in terms of *gameplay*.

We when talk about roleplaying games, we mean tabletop roleplaying games, like *Dungeons and Dragons* (for more on this, go to *Choose Your Own Adventure*). By definition, someone who intends to propose a roleplaying session to his friends has to have a scenario for them to play with.

An author's interests in preparing a RPG game are many. You use a universe or you build it yourself, you make the rules or follow the game's, you write a story with conflicts, challenges, consequences for a group's failure and rewards for their success. This group of players consists or your main characters and you, yourself, populate the scenario with secondary characters. It becomes quickly apparent, the roleplaying game scenario is a scenario all its own. So, it's an excellent exercise if you aspire to write stories for roleplaying game developers or if you aspire to pitch your own to them. In fact, writing a roleplaying game scenario and having someone play it is excellent practice.

An essential interest in this, aside from having a good, or bad, time – sometimes everything goes wrong – is getting direct feedback, whether positive or negative, from the group of players. At worst, these players are going to interact with your universe and your characters massively, and it's an excellent exercise in improvisation. This doesn't mean you have to invent a new story every second, but if your universe is coherent, the system of rules makes it credible, and if your secondary characters are good, you have everything necessary to redirect your players and, thus their characters, in the direction of your story. Although, yes, you can do something completely different. That's the power of RPGs. Sitting around a table, there are virtually no limits.

But in essence, an RPG interactive scenario has all the necessary elements, particularly the constraints, to offer an interactive story to players. If, for example, the plane can't be repaired, it can't be repaired.

All the difficulty with an RPG scenario is, thus, the interactive part of it. It means offering a story to one or more players. Be that as it may, RPG fans are familiar with two diametrically opposed stories: the linear story (for example, you flee down a long hallway, yes, it's all too linear) and what is referred to as the "sandbox" story (you're downtown, what do you do?) And even in the latter example, it's not just about managing a universe where the scriptwriter is free to introduce a story. This is what has given us MMORPGs.

However, your RPG scenario has some features that are particular to this type of creation. No, you don't have to foresee everything, that's impossible. Like an interactive scenario, you might say! The big difference is that with a RPG scenario, you don't write your players' dialogues, or their choices or corresponding responses. In fact, an RPG scenario has to give you what you need to interact with your players (or against them, if you happen to be particularly vengeful) to create, together, an RPG game, that unique experience that, on certain occasions, resembles an artistic performance, for good or ill. You might drop some scenes without a care for the sake of the story's coherence because you'll screw up everything in the meantime. In fact, the purpose of an RPG scenario is actually to be the element that lets you make the story, to roll it out and project it into your players' imaginations. But the story as written, save for the pushiest of linear stories, will never be the story that is played and lived.

However, if you write an interactive scenario for a video game, this inevitably defines the players' actions, not least because of the technique and *gameplay*. Unless you hack the game, or *cheat*, it's impossible. Similarly, for your part as a scriptwriter, you'll have selected and planned each possible interaction. True, in very developed games, you won't have to foresee whether the player is enjoying hopping about the village square for thirty minutes, but any action leading to an interaction with the story must be planned. If it is not, the player can't do anything, and she can only act based on the responses given. If you have to defeat a monster, it would be a fighting action, if you're playing a text-based game philosophizing with the Kant, you have to choose one of the proposed answers, or provide a game for philosophy master 2.

So, you can write an RPG interactive scenario with the elements described in this book, but always remember that determining the blocking for the players is tricky. However, if it's for your own game, you'll surely figure things out on D-day, however if it's to propose a scenario to other who are going to have other people playing it (the gamemasters), be twice as vigilant! You'll need to provide a few tricks to help this person in the event the players make some unsuitable choices, which means you have to have an excellent knowledge or the universe and the rules of the game you're writing for. As much as you can come up with a scenario on the fly with your storytelling talents, you have to sufficiently block a scenario to be used by a gamemaster, guide him, give him tips. It doesn't matter if he has the intention or rewriting your whole story: that's something you can't know in advance.

There is something particular you need to be aware about writing an RPG scenario and writing a scenario for another type of media: while an RPG inevitably teaches you how to cultivate your imagination, how to use it and restore it, remember what your boundaries are and what kind of RPG you're writing.

If I take a fun and fast RPG like *Manga BoyZ*, dividing the scenario into scenes is very clear, with one climax per scene, but the games are meant to be short; you won't find a structure consisting of acts or divided in sequences. On the other hand if you play *Torg, The Possibility Wars*, here you're going to need scriptwriting similar to a screenplay in terms of cutting. Take note: if the scriptwriting for an RPG is very formative, it is often very connected to the game universe and its rules.

Likewise, an RPG player may like to know the game universe down to the last detail, like the currency. If this doesn't serve your story, it has no place in a film or in your video game (for example, at any rate, when a player wants to buy something and there's no way to exchange money). It is important for a screen writer starting to write an RPG to learn to be concise in order to serve the story. Even if there are more liberties, by definition, in an interactive scenario for another medium, a screen writer must not forget that he cannot include everything and must propose an interactive narrative: something has to happen. The player isn't just there to admire how coherent your universe is, she's there to play.

Since *Dungeons and Dragons*, particularly in France where production is important both in terms of quantity and quality, the quality of RPG stories has clearly increased, if one is referring to the story rules. In fact, in their very essence, since RPGs allow everything, they are an ideal place to experiment with any type of scenario, even if it doesn't resemble a scenario. However, certain authors such as Johan Scipion, have acquired such a mastery of a certain scenario genre, slasher films in this particular case, *that each scenario of Sombre*[Shadow], his roleplaying game, is a lesson for anyone wishing to write about this topic.

Want some other roleplaying games?

- *Dungeons and Dragons* (fantasy)

- *Warhammer* (dark fantasy)

- *Paranoia* (dystopian Sci-Fi)

- *Shadowrun* (fantasy and cyberpunk)

- *Cyberpunk* (... cyberpunk)

- *Dark Heresy* (very, very dark Sci-Fi)

- Go to legrog.org (Guide du Rôliste Galactique [Galactic RPG Guide]), the largest Francophone database for RPGs, both French and foreign.

A brief word about *escape games*

Escape games are booming. The idea is that the player is set in certain space (submarine, prison, crime scene, etc.) and has to escape in a certain amount of time. The players are free, and like for tabletop roleplaying games, the choices are suggested by the universe. It's a matter of gathering clues, associating them and solving the riddle. All the ingredients are there: objective, urgency, cooperation, choice and consequences.

It's truly an interactive scenario. And like tabletop roleplaying games (and the notion of the sandbox), the player must take an active role to come out unharmed.

We would like to use some space in this book to focus on a company that has invented a new style of cross-genre storytelling.

It just goes to show that you can use anything, but fortunately there are many new forms yet to be invented.

In crossing genres, a blockbuster came our way thanks to the company Ici Même. It's entitled: *First Life*. In it, the player-spectator follows the steps of a character and lives an adventure in a city for about one hour. The game's title refers to *Second Life*, a "metaverse" (virtual universe) created in 2003 in which users, through their avatars, play as another person in a world they create and develop.

Here, the Other, the person you follow, and become if you're playing, is not something you get to choose, it's something you discover. And you don't see the person either, or at least very little, because you see things from the person's subjective point of view. In fact, the scenes in the story are viewed on a smart phone (where "smart" essentially means watching an uploaded video on a small screen in portrait layout). It's a long sequence shot of our character's subjective point of view. We see things through his eyes and his body is off camera.

An initial protocol, like a game rule (or "I" rule) for the game "to work," is thus necessary. You're provided a telephone and headphones and you're asked to let yourself be guided by the video. You hold the smart phone in your left hand. When the image does a panoramic shot to the right, you look to the right; when the image "moves forward" (travels), you move from place to place. When a hand appears on the screen, you do what the hand does: you open doors, you seize objects.

And so we move along by simply following an uploaded video, going from place to place and interacting with the real environment.

You have to put a certain trust in the screen writers of the story we've been given to live because the choices that are made are well and truly theirs. We're like passengers on a ghost train where the tracks are a film, the car is our own body and the haunted house, a journey into town, and we don't know where it's taking us or what will cross our paths. It is this gradual discovery of the places, the story and the person we incarnate who is "playing" and who creates the illusion that, as we have fun being this other person, these choices are really our own.

If you're writing a screenplay for audiovisual, go to
I'm writing for audiovisual!
If you're writing a scenario for radio, go to *I'm writing for radio!*
If you're writing a book, go to *I'm writing a book!*
If you're writing a cartoon, go to *I'm writing a comic book!*
If you're writing a video game, go to *I'm writing for a video game!*
Otherwise, go to *Everything begins at the ending!*

I'M WRITING FOR AUDIOVISUAL!

Unsurprisingly, it's film we dream about when we talk about scriptwriting. As you read through this book, it covers the key elements you need to write a screenplay. When it comes to writing one, interactive screenplays for television and cinema are still rare, though somewhat less for the Internet.

This alone shows how complex audiovisual interactive stories are. If you offer your viewers the chance to choose how the story develops by stopping the film during each sequence to propose choices, you inevitably have to make these sequences possible, even if, ultimately, only one will work for each branch.

It quickly becomes clear that the production time and cost will be crucial.

Here, we're talking about interactions where you don't have all the *gameplay* possible in a game, such as character management, etc. It's possible, but we also understand to what extent it will increase the budget and time needed for production.

You might say it's the same for a video game: the more stories, the more interactions, the more time and money you have to provide.

Always remember about film shooting.

You're not making a video to animate a story or capturing the actor's movements to render the character's motion fluid. You are shooting with a film crew and actors. And you're shooting all possible sequences.

Your interactive video scenario, we'll call it that, must be concrete... and supple at the same time. This is about making a video or a film, so there will be a director, and it probably won't be you. The director is going to have to manage the constraints, and one or another sequence may raise issues. However you, like your scenario, are responsible for the interactivity: the sequencing has to be logical. Thus, you have to make sure everything is shot or know how to do without something and figure out a solution without bringing your whole scenario crashing down.

We understand that it's tricky. It's even trickier if you don't shoot at a studio, or at least in an environment where you have control over everything, or almost everything. Because you have to shoot several sequences at a time, what the viewer's possible choices are, and what the player's precise choices are since she's the one interacting, there is a big risk you'll have continuity errors. Unless you subsequently plan to edit everything in post, you need to bear this risk in mind when everything changes around you (the sea, the road in the back, the factory, the crowd, etc.) The shadow of a cloud is enough to give you a continuity error with the lighting.

Obviously, if your player/viewer sees everything from a subjective viewpoint, and thus makes choices for herself or for the character she is playing as, it will be even more different if everything is in third person. This requires a big effort from the actor playing the hero to act out a sequence with these different successive subtleties. And pay good attention to the actor's costume, what he's wearing, etc.

Don't neglect the transitions! If the player/viewer can move about or make the hero move about at different points, you have to think about how you're going to introduce these transitions into your scenario: this can't consist of just fades to black and ellipses. Note that this is an overriding issue if you are shooting for *virtual reality*[3] (VR).

Along this train of thought, though this will have consequences for your whole scenario, try as best as you can to be familiar with the shooting locations and take part in the scouting. When you write an interactive scenario, if the director has to work himself out of a jam with your story based on the locations ultimately chosen for shooting, there may be some constraints he'll manage to overcome – that's his job – but will he be mindful of the scenario's architecture to make sure everything is coherent if he makes a change?

....

3. Or virtual reality in French. This is an experience with a helmet equipped with a screen covering your face that allows you to move your head slightly in a 3D video game simulation or a film shot in 360° video. The point of view (in the literal sense) is, thus, totally free, hence the challenge to the narration, the art of point of view (in the figurative sense).

Because we're talking about an interactive scenario: more than ever, the director has to be mindful of the fact that any change can have consequences beforehand and afterwards – the hitch is that there are several beforehand and afterwards, this time. And here you have to be spot on. A director knows that you rarely shoot a film in a linear manner, and he's used to shooting multiple takes to get the right one. With your sequences, take care to point out what changes from one sequence to another so he doesn't have to wonder whether he's needlessly repeating a take. Conversely, dialogue with the director: he may notice a sequence was needlessly repeated, and everyone saves time by deleting.

Again, to reinforce this point on the difficulty of interactive audiovisual stories, remember that you hardly ever get the chance to do a second shoot. If there is an error in your story, or an issue involving starting over, it's hard to fix it. These are the rushes you'll have to work around. Editors can work miracles, but editing film from an interactive scenario requires great discipline.

The problem with an audiovisual interactive scenario can be bypassed by only shooting the sequence that the audience would have chosen. Obviously, in this case, you're not delivering a complete interactive audiovisual product. An online series offering the fans the choice to vote on the next episode can, in this way, interest viewers and increase their loyalty. But let's not veer too far from interactivity because the fans that didn't choose the most voted choice can't live the adventure they wished to. This isn't an interactive scenario, it's more like an interactive synopsis, where you write the sequence as you go. Which may look like time saved to the scriptwriter, but everything will depend on how the film crew reacts.

By way of example, you may be interested in the series *Tantale* (http://tantale. nouvelles-ecritures.francetv.fr/). This will give you a good idea.

There is also *Late Shift*, an interactive film written by Tobias Weber and Michael Robert Johnson. The film is worth checking out because it was filmed using *full motion video*.

> If you're writing a scenario for a roleplaying game, go to *I'm writing for a roleplaying game!*
> If you're writing a scenario for radio, go to *I'm writing for radio!*
> If you're writing a book, go to *I'm writing a book!*
> If you're writing a cartoon, go to *I'm writing a comic book!*
> If you're writing a video game, go to *I'm writing for a video game!*
> Otherwise, go to *Everything begins at the ending!*

Cinema and video games, the *crossover!*

Benjamin, what was the success of Beyond: Two Souls *like for you?*

Benjamin Diebling: *Beyond* has given me a lot of little things I've experienced since then. After shooting *Beyond*, I was very lucky, I was selected by my school to represent French cinema in Australia, where I went to do a master's in writing and cinematography. Going back to school after *Beyond* was really weird, but I realized that the work methods on set had given me discipline and confidence. However, it was when I came back to work on *Detroit* that I realized that, more than anything, *Beyond* had given me the ability to think quickly and navigate all the choices, the variations in a character's story, in a scene and in an environment following the choices.

In interactive storytelling, how does one direct actors who are accustomed to acting in linear storytelling?

The director and the actor can make suggestions. It's like a game, you often go back over the writing. That gives a lot of freshness to the characters. Plus, directing is pretty easy because we work with professional actors who can change from one sentiment to another quickly, all the while maintaining the same tension, the same intensity in their acting.

How do you guide your actors in building a character that is always evolving?

It's quite complex. Since one character can become a hero just as easily as a piece of garbage based on the player's choices, we think about two different characters. They both have the same background, the same history, but they become two different characters. Generally, we do several days of shooting for the actor to play the "bad guy," then we do the same for the "good guy." Sometimes, the actor has to play both characters on the same day for practical reasons (a set or an actor is available for only one day, etc.) In this case, it's up to the director to direct the actor so he plays both roles correctly. We tend to choose actors who have the ability to change roles.

I'M WRITING FOR RADIO!

This time, seeing isn't required. Here, you're in quite a different setup, it's the only genre of its kind. Thus, there are some very specific constraints. Obviously, you can forget the scenery, the lighting, the facial expression, the body language... In summary, you just need to focus on the sound, the intonation, and the words.

But you have to write an interactive scenario. That means, then, that your player will have to make decisions based on what she has heard, and that alone. There is a challenge, here, for the player: her ability to pay attention.

Naturally, we think of blind or visually impaired people as the audience for this kind of scenario, so be very careful if this is really your audience: you're going to be writing an audio interactive scenario for an audience who perceives the world differently than you.

It will be much easier to write for the general public, i.e. people who can see. With the knowledge that you'll undoubtedly have another challenge: the ability to pay attention.

A player always needs to be attentive, but, in this case, she can use all of her available senses. In a radio-based game (it can also be on a smart phone, podcast, etc.), the player only uses her hearing. Thus, you first have to find out what conditions she'll be playing in (in transportation, at home, at a audio gaming room?). Everything depends on the ability to pay attention. If it is not possible to re-listen to a scene, then we suggest you allow a reduced period of time for making a decision on the other choice. As you can see, with this type of scenario, we are already inside the game mechanics, inside the *gameplay*, because it is very particular.

Once you have incorporated this notion of attentive listening, calibrate your scenes. Most of the information will come from the actors; you need to provide a crystal-clear script. For the rest, your best friend will be the sound engineer, and he must also have a clear vision of the project. Consequently, the director has to look out for all of this. As with audiovisual, everything will be acted out, though not at a film shoot, but rather at a recording session. You can spare yourself from worrying about the continuity errors, but be mindful of the soundscape: if the sound engineer errs, you'll lose coherence. And if you have the flexibility to correct a scene – even if it takes more time and money – and if it's easier to consider recording an audio scene again, bear in mind however that you'll only be able to use what's already been recorded. This is preferable.

As you can see, the process has one point in common with audiovisual: when you produce the substance of the game, your scenario has to be impeccable because it will be very hard to go over it again later.

Tips for recording with actors

If you are present during the recording session, pay attention to how the actors "energy" connects between takes. If you can, pause and listen back to make sure that, despite the preceding choices, the consistency is really there.

Be attentive to the how the emotion at the end of scene connects (for example, hate) with the emotion of that starts the following scene (a good laugh). A brusque change from one emotion to another can lead to an error in continuity. One trick that helps is to bring in supporting characters in order to make the transition smoother.

As well, careful with last-minute ideas. You'll no doubt get the urge to redo a dialogue, change its pace, on occasion to make sure the feeling is just right... However, with interactive storytelling, one slight change can make an entire branch incoherent. It can often be frustrating, but when recording, focus on making the best of what you already have.

Audio-only interactive games are rare. You can try *A Blind Legend*, which is pay to play and completely designed for a non-seeing audience, or *Audigame*, a free compilation of twelve small adventures.

If you're writing a scenario for a roleplaying game, go to *I'm writing for a roleplaying game!*

If you're writing a scenario for audiovisual, go to *I'm writing for audiovisual!*

If you're writing a book, go to *I'm writing a book!*

If you're writing a cartoon, go to *I'm writing a comic book!*

If you're writing a video game, go to *I'm writing for a video game!*

Otherwise, go to *Everything begins at the ending!*

I'M WRITING A BOOK!

One medium that was a massive hit in the 1980s was none other than the "choose your own adventure" book (Go to Choose Your Own Adventure books), also called CYOA.

First off, you cannot exclude the reader's age when conceptualizing your interactive story. The reader's age has become a point of obsession at book stores and publishing houses, with the use of concepts such as young adult or cross-over literature.

And like anything else, an audiovisual product can be prohibited for a certain group of spectators, including minors, because in publishing there is a law from 1949, which governs publications intended for minors. You simply can't write anything you want, and make no mistake, while the law has been around since 1949, you can see on *legifrance.fr* that it's update regularly. Video game developers are covered by the Pan European Game Information[4] (PEGI), but PEGI is not a law.

Why talk about age and, *in sum*, youth? Because the Choose Your Own Adventure book, or the gamebook, is first and foremost intended for a young audience.

By gamebook, we also often refer to albums, some of them well illustrated books, intended for a young audience, such as *La jungle aux 100 pièges* [The Jungle of 100 Pitfalls] from Grind. The number 100 in the title is not without meaning. Indeed, since an interactive scenario allows virtually anything, and, by definition, a book is a finite object unable to contain an infinite quantity (at least compared to a computer), your story is going to have to hold up over 100 pages, 100 paragraphs, etc.

It's an inconvenience, you're limited; it's an advantage, you have boundaries.

Traditionally, ever since the first Choose Your Own Adventure book *The Warlock of Firetop Mountain*, CYOA sets a limit of 400 paragraphs for teens, or young adults as we say nowadays. Why 400? It's not rocket science. The author, Steve Jackson, can easily explain for you. At a conference put on by Gallimard Jeunesse on the initiative of publisher Le Grimoire, Steve Jackson explained, in a humor one could describe as British, explained that he had written 399 paragraphs and aesthetically, he didn't like it.

You'll note that we're talking about Gallimard Jeunesse, a historic French publisher of choose your own adventure books, part of whose name, Jeunesse (Youth), indicates who the their target audience is. However, the young players

....

4. PEGI is a age-based video game classification system recognized throughout Europe that allows parents and children, for example, to choose games best suited to their age. Among other things, it allows you to know whether a game has sensitive content (violence, sex, etc.) or if the game incorporations a monetization system.

of thirty years ago have grown up. And, if out of nostalgia, some may like replaying their old books, unless you're deliberately stamping your work as a "revival" or "in the great tradition," you can no longer produce the same stories of the great era, especially if your targeting an older audience.

When Le Grimoire, a veritable laboratory on the subject, offers *La Geste de Gurdil [Gurdil's Gest]* to the public, though everything outwardly resembles a classic quest of fantasy, a very common topic in choose-your-own-adventure books, the very topic of the quest, the conflicts put forth and the characters are mindful of the fact thirty years have passed.

If, before, a reader was happy to discover a fantasy universe, nowadays, there it's very likely your reader has already heard of these universes, given the films about them. In a certain way, while a CYOA makes use of one genre, remember that this is a genre all of its own, and, as with all genres, be wary of the clichés and know how to use them right. Your mastery of the genre's codes will you do play off them, and your player will easily forgive your deviations. Remember, too, that writing a genre makes it easier to grip the reader and, on your end, the choices, it must be said, to be made when conceptualizing your story. A reader will want to play a fantasy, sciencefiction, or adventure story before she'll want to play a choose-your-own-adventure story.

In terms of writing, tackling a choose-your-own-adventure book is an excellent way to tackle interactive storytelling. Right away, unless you're working for a license, you don't have to incorporate a whole roleplaying game universe – one can often consider, too, that it's a good way to get started with roleplaying games. For your book, you will have a universe, rules, one (or perhaps some) character(s), a story, all limited to the book, whereas a roleplaying game stretches the limits.

Define your number of paragraphs – maybe you don't have enough material or maybe you'll have to shorten your story – because this boundary, in such a simple *gameplay*, will allow you tackle or refine the interactive scriptwriting.

Note that, when writing your story, you'll undoubtedly have a need for some paragraphs for unique choices. In theory, each paragraph is supposed to propose several choices to the player because if she's happy just rolling dice to pass a test, her interactivity is rather limited. But since it's a book, in your writing you'll undoubtedly be forced to send the player back to a paragraph with only one choice because you need a stage where you tie up your story's loose ends or resolve the plot. You need to avoid this as much as possible because each one-choice paragraph is, by its nature, not interactive, even though it's a technical constraint.

In the end, if you needed convincing to write this kind of work, a choose-your-own-adventure has a limited number of paragraphs, and that's going to force you to limit your number of endings. You'll see in the part in question, it's not insignificant to know that you have *n* paragraphs: this forces you to discipline yourself.

As for your player, you'll have to assume she'll play fair. Indeed, since everything is in the book, all you have to do is navigate from one paragraph to another to go back, or just flip through the pages to find the solution. You can be clever, but if the player is determined to cheat, she'll get away with it. We will note that a player who asks other players for help is not "cheating": it's another way for a community of players to experience your story. What's more, it's quite possible the original cheater may subsequently share the solutions. This is like everything else in the digital age, it's up to the player to decide whether or not she's going to do the right thing or not.

For people not familiar with these books, here are some perfect examples of paragraphs from *La Geste de Gurdil*. As you'll see, it's all very simple:

A one-choice paragraph example: "[...] Not only did you not catch up to him, but when you look around... You realize you're completely lost! To resolve this go to page **170**."

A multiple-choice paragraph: "[...] So, what will your strategy be? If you try themain entrance, go to page **254**. If you try the side entrance, go to page **308**. If not, do you turn around and depart for the fourth site of your map? If so, go to page **382**. You can also get some exercise and go over the palisade. If so, go to page **351**."

Here's an example of a paragraph where one relies on the player to play fair, even though nothing is forcing her to give the right answer after rolling a die"[...] If you roll, go to page **30**; 2, go to page **54**; 3, go to page **73**; 4, go to page **177**; 5, go to page **211** and if 6, go to page **325**."

If you're writing a scenario for a roleplaying game, go to
I'm writing for a roleplaying game!
If you're writing a scenario for audiovisual, go to
I'm writing for audiovisual!
If you're writing a scenario for radio, go to *I'm writing for radio!*
If you're writing a cartoon, go to *I'm writing a comic book!*
If you're writing a video game, go to *I'm writing for a video game!*
Otherwise, go to *Everything begins at the ending!*

I'M WRITING A COMIC BOOK!

Interactive comic books exist. It's based on the same principle as the choose-your-own-adventure books, sending the reader to the page of her choice, or choices. One can also use the term *visual novel*. It's more chic, and the notion of a screen is more apparent in the name when the comic book is in digital format. However, to our mind, a *visual novel* is going to be more similar to a video game. In this part, we'll be talking, in particular, about physical comic books.

We could have included gamebook-style albums here, but these have full-page illustrations like choose-your-own-adventure books and are not divided into strips with boxes. While the album-style gamebook often uses illustration as the *gameplay* (the solution to the riddle is in the picture), as opposed to choose-your-own-adventure books, which limit it to a decorative role (though sometimes they contain riddles), graphically, and in the narrative, interactive comic books offer more interaction with the pictures.

In France, you can consult works published by Makaka. Below are some titles that are currently available as we write this book:

- *Mystery, la BD dont vous êtes le super-héros [Mysterya, the Choose Your Own Adventure Comic Book]*
- *Sherlock Holmes et le défi d'Irène Adler [Sherlock Holmes and the Challenge of Irene Adler]*
- *Hold-up, journal d'un braqueur [Holdup, the Diary of a Bankrobber]*
- *Zombies*

As you can see, there are many different genres.

Consequently, the story topics are the same as they are for books, with an added advantage, however, that you need to consider for your interactive scenario: for one drawing alone, you may have scenery that requires lines and lines of description. Which means the picture shouldn't be overloaded: evoking the idea of an uncluttered world in the mind of your reader doesn't require any less lines of writing than describing a Hindu fresco does sometimes.

Consequently, as with an album-style gamebook, think of visual power of the picture. You may often have better control than with possible for audiovisual (complicated filming, costly special effects, etc.) On the other hand, the action won't flow as well as a video game.

One of the key elements of your interactive scenario is to reflecting on when to send a reader to a strip or a box. It's easy to understand: sending the reader to boxes offers more choices, but the visual effect will be more limited. Do not use a full strip if you don't plan on including interactive elements (city map, labyrinth, etc.)

When sending the reader to a box, you have a choice to make. Either your boxes are sprinkled throughout the strips, at the risk of losing aestheticism, or you boxes send the reader to other boxes on the same strip, and in a glance, your player can see the different possible consequences – even if you send the action between two strips facing each other. Interactive comic books require a little more fair-play from the player than books.

If you're thinking comic books, also think about the seventh art. If your interactive comic book can serve as a good foundation, you should subsequently produce an audiovisual interactive scenario. But that will require development all the same. Don't forget that, unless you're making a gigantic album, you'll be limited by the number of strips. Have a good look at current productions to see how many strips the scriptwriters and illustrators are using.

Lastly, never forget that a comic book is an object, even more than a book. That's why the atmosphere of your story must jump out from the pages as soon as your reader picks it up.

If you're writing a scenario for a roleplaying game, go to
I'm writing for a roleplaying game!
If you're writing a scenario for audiovisual, go to
I'm writing for audiovisual!
If you're writing a scenario for radio, go to *I'm writing for radio!*
If you're writing a book, go to *I'm writing a book!*
If you're writing a video game, go to *I'm writing for a video game!*
Otherwise, go to *Everything begins at the ending!*

I'M WRITING FOR A VIDEO GAME!

This is a domain that is sure to generate a large number of interactive stories. If you haven't already done so, we recommend you first go to *I'm writing for a roleplaying game!* Several items may help you.

This domain is vast and the technical limitations in terms of computers are infinitely less demanding, if we may exaggerate a little. Soon, the only limit will be the scriptwriter's imagination, hence the importance of knowing your work well, so your scenario can be a prop for the imaginary, a real springboard, instead of a straitjacket. This is where the difficulty will lie: guiding, steering and proposing a story/stories without the player feeling restrained.

This is the main goal of this book, writing an interactive scenario for video games. Text-based video games, including choose-your-own-adventure books, are by nature based on an interactive scenario. Narrative-based video games offer a different experience yet they're based on the same structure, the interactive scenario. MMORPGs are brimming with quests and interactive stories, but could it be that these stories are getting lost in such a vast metastory that the player's experience might, ironically, come to be summed up by an accumulation of experience points.

There has to be a story or stories. You're doing to create an arborescence, the players will jump from branch to branch or explore one of them that leads to the top of the tree, but they'll be able to share stories born of this tree, they will have lived a common *and* personalized experience. The immersive force of a video game led by a good interactive story is a beautiful experience; your scenario must permit it.

True, all other kinds of media aim for a quality experience, but the power of video games in this regard is all too real. A technical power, to be sure, visual, audio, and now in virtual reality, however it is a temporary power. What do we mean by that?

The duration of the game is both the most complicated factor to assess and also an key factor. We will come back this.

We are alluding to the ability to "lose yourself" in MMORPGs, to see the story become diluted – this is connected to the virtually infinite game time that these video games offer. You, as a scriptwriter, offer a story. In interactive storytelling, there is interaction, of course, but more than anything there is storytelling. And whoever says interactive story well and truly means story. Your story has a beginning, middle, and an ending, and you makes those plural for an interactive scenario, except for the beginning sometimes. What you have to understand is that this book is going to tell you or remind you what the key elements are so you can captivate and retain your player. And the first rule is to have a story, and the difference with vast MMORPGs, where virtual boredom, a virtually infinite boredom, is always lying in wait, is that the video game writer must bear the fourth dimension, i.e. time, well in mind. Everything has a purpose.

In technical terms, a scriptwriter already working with a team has to really bear in mind what a character can and cannot do, and research the developers' abilities to, precisely, develop or not specific actions. You don't write a monster chase in a forest the same way you do a paranormal investigation in the middle of a city.

If you're making a story-based video game, research whether the game engine uses a trigger-event system, how it works, etc. Sometimes, it's better to ask obvious questions than to have to start all over because everyone thought everyone knew. Likewise, don't limit yourself if a certain situation is not provided for. Always ask the question: what you may consider to be complicated to develop may be very simple, and vice-versa.

Do you want to write an interactive scenario but don't have a team? Nothing's impossible, someone has to begin the story, right? On the other hand, you're going to have to give serious consideration to *gameplay* and anything dealing with the games mechanics. This book is here for that, too. We live in a time of impressive video game capabilities, and it's not going to stop here. If you build a good interactive scrip, it's very unlikely that any technical problems will be insurmountable. After that, it's like everything else, time and money are two factors that will guide your writing. Doing away with both is a luxury only few scriptwriters can afford.

If you're writing a scenario for a roleplaying game, go to
I'm writing for a roleplaying game!
If you're writing a scenario for audiovisual, go to
I'm writing for audiovisual!
If you're writing a scenario for radio, go to *I'm writing for radio!*
If you're writing a book, go to *I'm writing a book!*
If you're writing a cartoon, go to *I'm writing a comic book!*
Otherwise, go to *Everything begins at the ending!*

PRO INSIGHT

Erwan, can you tell us, for an author, what interactive scriptwriting means as an opportunity?

Erwan Le Breton: It depends a little on what kind of author you are. Based on my own experience, and on the profiles of I've already interacted with, I've come up with several categories.

First, there are the "kings of structure," who are very gifted at coming up with a story with twists, which works very well for both linear stories and stories with branches. For them, the idea of moving toward interactivity is great because that allows them to say, "I create my main story and then I imagine the branches, 'and what if, an what if, what if.'" This allows you to create a tree, as if you were writing the same story several times with all the alternate paths. Marc Marti, a professor of narratology the University of Nice Sophia Antipolis, uses an expression I really like to describe these story branches that could have existed but aren't apparent in classic, linear fiction. He calls this "phantom stories."

Another kind is the "dialogue writer." Dialogue writers are writers who really know how to give a character a voice. You recognize these guys right away because they have characters who are very particular because of the way they talk. For them, interactive writing leads them to imagine several variants of one dialogue, but they remain focused on the character, its voice, etc. So, it's not necessarily a complete change of mindset If you're a good dialogue writer, you can work on anything, a comic book, a film, a video game... In the end, whether there's interactivity or not really doesn't change much.

A third kind is the "descriptive" writer. Descriptive writers are capable of evoking a scene for you and having you feel emotion for the power of the words; they have a style all their own, they really go an set a tone, an atmosphere, a scene... These writers are generally novelists. With audiovisual, this isn't where they usually shine the brightest, because the picture, the sound and the music are generally going to replace their work. With video games, there are also text-based adventure games, where you'll often find some very evocative passages. For this kind of author, interactivity isn't necessarily what's going to interest them or help them the most, and it's certainly not them who we're going to seek out in the first place. But they're not incompatible either.

Another category of author I often find are the "*world-builders*," who don't necessarily know how to write well-structured stories, or very good dialogue, but they have a very good notion of context. They'll define a very coherent framework governed by rules that have a big narrative impact, sometimes with a unique appeal. There are novels, films and games you finish by saying: "Whoa, that wasn't written so well, the characters were a little generic, the dialogue a little dull, the plot predictable, but that world is incredible!" For this kind of author, interactivity is more the emergence of an open world because they're going to create a context that is overflowing with story opportunities.

If we go outside the classic definition of the writer, there is a new profile emerging in a lot of video games. It's the "*narrative designer*." We could call it something different, but I use this term to designate authors who immediately think in terms of a decision trees, story structures with narrative moments, which aren't necessarily linked to each other in a linear, chronologically scripted manner. Instead of thinking of narration in terms of pages filled with words, descriptions and stage directions, they think in terms of *mind maps* with the possibilities and outlines, or in terms of tables with columns, lists and conditions. This is a new kind of author that we could describe as a "native" to interactivity. It's a profile that now has a place, now more than ever, in the world of entertainment, for video games, but also for choose-your-own-adventure books, interactive fiction, etc.

That being said, these categories are not set in stone. An author can be very at ease in many domains. And above all, regardless of the writer's profile, you have something to contribute to the interactive narrative. This can help you play with your "art" or your means of expression and boost what you thought you were capable of doing. It's a little as if tomorrow we said to a classical or rock guitarist: "You're going to do some free jazz." At first, he's going to say, "Oh my God!" and, then, gradually he'll discover a new universe of possibilities where the rules can be bent or broken.

However, not everyone finds that interesting. There are some who turn to stone thinking about it. It's also a mindset, you have to love pursuing kinds of things.

3. PREPARING YOURSELF FOR INTERACTIVE WRITING

EVERYTHING BEGINS AT THE END!

When you start a novel, a short story, or even a scenario, you can very grab a blank sheet of paper, you iPad or your keyboard and get going.

It's the best way to unbalance your interactive scenario or never finish it. Every interactive narrative, a bit like crime novels of old, must begin at the end: how did we get here? And when we talk of interactivity, we're talking of multiple endings or, at least, many paths to arrive at the end.

You will be personalizing players' experience if you offer different endings because they will all live a different ending from among the array of possibilities you offered.

However, no, you don't have to think in terms of endings to find your story. You certainly need an idea for a beginning, several if possible, come up with a topic, all of which will fill out your story. But as soon as you feel like you have enough material, you need to start visualizing the endings. You can see: the more endings you have, the more different they are, the more paths leading there involve radical decisions from the player, the more complex your interactive scenario will be

For a classic narrative – by classic we mean non-interactive – the difficulty of your work is going to be determining your choices in order to reduce your story to one plot. You will abandon ideas, characters, places, etc.

To help you choose your number of endings in a way other than rolling a die, think right away about the stories you can weave around your main plot. Logically, if you have a viable story, it's possible to develop it with a classic narrative. In this case, instead of eliminating the variants of your story, briefly imagine which endings could come to pass if this or that happened. From a practical standpoint, obviously, one of the most obvious endings is the death or your character, or at least his failure if you don't kill the hero or heroin of the story. There are already number variants of possible failures.

Offering different paths ending in failure to arrive at the end is a good way to tackle writing an interactive scenario if you've never done one before. Thereafter, you'll begin to get to the heart of interactive storytelling by offering other endings besides death or failure. "And what if..." the player opted for such or such decision at such moment? You will see, this involves certain building rules, but for now let's focus on the endings.

A classic move is to visualize two main endings. In one, the player has chosen the path of good, in the other, the path or evil, and the latter is not a failure, a moral failure perhaps, but it isn't recognized as *game over*. If you add to this all the endings where the heroin fails, you'll already have quite a bit of work, a multitude of "sudden deaths" and two main endings.

Next, you ramp things up by offering different main endings. At first glance, you can remain Manichean, but offer gradations in success. There is a difference between being the boss of the group of heros, the director of the league of heros and the Great Savior of humanity. Just as being a ringleader is not as important as being a dictator or finishing as a galactic Emperor. Here, you already have six different endings.

Do you want to come out on the side of good or evil? Imagine a management game where, in the end, you'll be homeless, city mayor, director of the hospital, etc. We can explore many possibilities, but be careful unless you're making a *serious game*, and even then, never neglect morality in an interactive narrative.

This is what will engage the player the most. We will come back to this point. And if, to begin, you are at least able to visualize a turning point with a Cornelian choice, it needs to be a short experience where the player doesn't have too much time, and she knows it, to take interest in the psychological and moral aspect. However, a brutal change in a longer experience will come as a surprise, and no doubt for the worse. You need to distill the points where the player, based on her choices, will ultimately decide on such or such direction.

Benjamin, how does one successfully reroute the story to keep the game production from skyrocketing?

Benjamin Diebling: In roleplaying games, we let the possibilities get out of hand. There are all types of endings, but with lots of nuances. It's up to the gamemaster's discretion. He has to improvise with the consequences. That's what makes roleplaying games unique. In a video game, it's different. In *Heavy Rain* or *Detroit*, we created a whole park with whole characters. We write them, we film them and we produce them graphically even if the player will notice 10% of it. However, you have to limit them and rationalize your ideas: a character in the story who comes to help the player after a series of choices can be reused at another time, following another series of choices. It's not always necessary to create two characters if one can be used in several combinations. You need to combine the characters and the ideas in paths that don't cross.

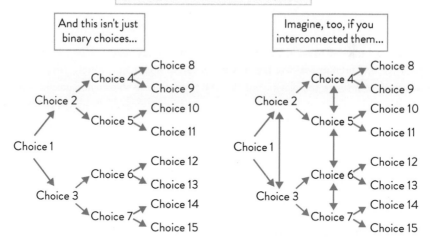

Why you need to think about endings: the danger of a combinatorial explosion

And this isn't just binary choices...

Imagine, too, if you interconnected them...

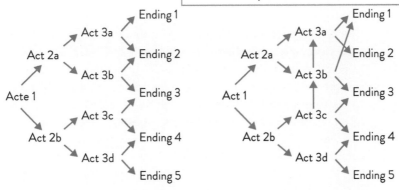

Defining the endings allows you to guide the choices

You can see already that Endings 1 and 5 are, in theory, less common.

Here, we redirect things toward Ending 1. If you don't have any idea about the endings, you can't do it.

TEMPUS FUGIT

Time is a frequent topic in this book because it is a key factor. True, this is the case for any human activity, but in your case, it's about how much game time you wish to offer to the player, but also the time you are able to dedicate to the project.

This last point is a little taboo, but yes, we only have so much time to write. The reasons are many and varied, but even someone writing a book about the life of someone like J.R.R. Tolkien only has so much time to dedicate the book. And while J.R.R. Tolkien considered his work to be unfinished, he published some books allowing access to his work.

If you are an author who works on the side to make ends meet, someone who has a "real job" as they say, what you "really do," your time, like J.R.R. Tolkien's, is limited each week. There's a reason one often find teachers in the field of writing – the possibility to have set, extended vacation to write is a considerable advantage. And plus, a pinch of skill in reading and writing never hurts.

And if you don't have another job besides writing, unless you've achieved G.R.R. Martin status, to use the example of a "modern Tolkien," you need money to survive, which generates the typical stress people get when they have to make ends meet, and, between the lean times and an overloaded calendar, time manager is essential.

In this respect, we can hardly help you. There is only one watchword: discipline. Only you can make yourself sit down at your desk to write. Whether your a morning person, a night person, someone who works at a café, with a cat on you lap, etc., it's up to you to decide.

You're going to write a story consisting of stories, in which a player is going to interact. You think about your endings and you're going to have to get them right, while at the same time offering interesting game paths. Don't go thinking that you can write, let's say, 10% of the text, and then you come back two months later to do another 20%, then resume three weeks later, etc. That's possible for a linear narrative; you reread the preceding passage, you resume, you reread your notes and recommence; normally you're going toward the same ending and if you go off course, you'll adapt the story with brio.

With interactive storytelling, you're going to be dealing with several stories at the same time, plus all the nuances of each one. Your memory, and we'll go so far as to talk as if it were a computer with random access memory, is going to be called upon a lot. And if you empty your random access memory to do something else and resume much too later, it will be complicated to go back over the roads traveled, to reread and understand your notes, to see where you wanted to get to and how you planned to do it. Once we've determined all the preliminary elements of an interactive scenario, we write it in one go. That means in the least amount of interrupted days possible.

Obviously, you will find yourself at a crossroads of possibilities, like when writing a linear narrative. But instead of abandoning choices and taking *one* direction, you'll have to select *some* choices, take *some* directions, etc. These moments will force you to stop writing to think about the scenario and check where you're at; you'll need to take good note of the options you selected. Because when you resume writing soon after, you'll only be able to deal with one branch after another. When writing an interactive scenario, you can almost literally lose your way.

Hence, managing your time well. If you have a *deadline*, you may dedicate too much time to the first option; in developing it too much, you make a main plot that few players will abandon to explore subplots, the development of which will be shorter, for the very simple reason that you will have had less time to deal with them. In reality, this disparity in almost inevitable, and if all the paths don't perhaps all have the same game time, you need to make sure they aren't too disproportionate, unless you're doing so deliberately for certain choices. Indeed, if we've clearly told the player not to press the red button and she does it, everything stops for your character...

When you work on one of the story's directions, take a good look at how much time your dedicate to it and evaluate how much time you have left for the others. In general, as a scriptwriter, and thus as a human, you will favor the paths that stimulate you the most. Always remember that the player may have other tastes or different habits than you: be careful not to devalue any moral choices you may loathe, for example, by unconsciously limiting the player's interactivity. Be especially careful if you are completing a work order that's not exactly your cup of tea; there are specifications you have to respect. As a good professional, you will bear them in mind.

So, keep an eye on your stop-watch. Over time, if we may go so far, you will learn to gauge your working time just right. In a way, it's easier than for a novel or short story because you're writing for a game, so you'll have to implement the game's mechanics well, you'll have to submit the part of the scenario you're working on before replacing it.

Don't have a *deadline*? Is it a personal project? No matter the reason, no one is going to come asking for your copy at scheduled time. Thus, you may never finish. Here, we're talking about interactive scriptwriting. Imagine if J.R.R. Tolkien said to himself that he wanted to make *Lord of the Rings* a choose-your-own-adventure book. He probably never would have finished it. Set yourself a *deadline*, and when you get close to it, take a look where you're at, see if you're getting close to the endings of your story or not. Is it worth pushing the deadline back? Or are you going to procrastinate? With the knowledge that we're well in agreement: while the discipline to write is essential to writing a scenario, there are days where things don't come, where your neurons freeze up. You'll also learn, if you haven't already, to differentiate between a lazy period, where you just need to call upon your discipline, and a period of reflection or fatigue, where it's better to change ideas, do something else, while you're brain works in the background. If you force your writing too much, your imagination is going to go after whatever is simplest, the clichés, and your work may take an unsavory turn. Organizing your time also means bearing in mind your human nature.

And always remember: the gaming experience you want to offer is also game time. You can offer thirty different endings if the branches leading there take 3 minutes of game time. It is important to inform the player ahead of time before she plays and probably pays for a very, very short experience. Replayability is thus fundamental.

However, in building your arborescence, remember that your working time is the game time. If you offer a scene that ends with 28 choices followed by 28 different scenes, writing 28 possibilities is going to take you some time, while the player will only play only one of them... This, too, is what this book is going to teach you to manage.

Time is work for you and fun for the player.

PRO INSIGHT

Careful with time!

David, how long do you take to write an interactive story?

David Cage: Way too much time, if you ask my friends and family! Writing a game like *Heavy Rain* took me an entire year, working full time, sometimes 6 to 7 days a week. *Detroit* took me twice as long to write, something like two and a half years.

Erwan, are there any specific time constraints for interactive scriptwriting?

Erwan Le Breton: There is a cost to an interactive scenario, that's the reality. You have a great story in mind. First, you write it linearly, but then you imagine several possible choices. You're going to multiply your development costs by 3, 4, 5, 10. And you put money toward the interactivity, you're going to have to put less elsewhere. You're going to offer shorter experiences, or at a less sustainable pace.

Take for example a 2-hour action film where something is always happening. If you add narrative choices, with the same budget, you're going to have to condense the experience, and it'll maybe last an hour or less, but with *replay value* for its replayability. Conversely, you can "dilute" your plot to create an open world that offers 100 hours where, unfortunately however, there will be moments of pause, repetitions, etc. But actually that's not a problem. Because you're noting going to use up all this content in one go right off the bat, and also because you'll appreciate the moments of pause. If it were 100 hours at break-neck speed, you'd have the impression you were at a *death metal* concert with nonstop *shredding*. I think after a while, even if you're a fan of the genre, you can't keep up. In music, silence is important and so are the pauses, the crescendos, the decrescendos, and all the changes in rhythm. It's the same for storytelling.

Joe, how do you manage your writing time?

Joe Pinney: I work as hard as possible without missing out on the rest of my life. Occasionally, I succeed.

Thomas, how do you manage the consequences of the player's actions?

Thomas Veauclin: Just by having time ahead of you. You establish an action. From here, you envision all the expected logical reactions. Of all the possible ones, you check whether they enter into your plans. Can you produce them? If yes, that's all there is. If not, you have to find other less costly solutions or not put the player in that situation.

If you are interested in the history of an interactive scenario, go to *The interactive scenario, a history of a revamped genre.*
If you want to see or see again how to write a scenario, go to *Interactive story fundamentals.*
If you like getting your hands dirty, go to *The mechanics of interactivity.*
But just before that, we offer you a little help on how to get organized. Go to *How to prepare your work.*

PRO INSIGHT

Jean-Luc, do you go back over your story, contrary to a classic narrative, where you write and submit your work?

Jean-Luc: Yes, I redo passages. I'm almost always rewriting. The foundation doesn't change, but the scenes evolve. We rewrite them almost all the time, we tweak them. But you always have to remember to make sure the story is consistent and keep the most important scenes and tie up the loose ends.

HOW TO PREPARE YOUR WORK

A methodology

We offer you a methodology. It's up to you find inspiration in it or create your own: the important thing is that it works!

The reservoir

This is a document where we put, at random, all the scenes this story evokes in us. In fact, it so happens that after you define your hero's main goal, we get trapped rather quickly. The reservoir consists of notes, ideas, surprises. *What can I do with my character that would surprise me?*

This is also the moment to surpass your masters. The reservoir can be used as anteroom, for example when you get inspired by a scene, you're going to twist it and transform it to serve your purposes.

The step outline

It is advisable to write using a step outline, which gathers all of the big plot lines in your story. This contains all of the main scenes and the branches. This document is very important because allows you to lay the first pieces of the puzzle.

Don't be stingy in describing each sequence. This document must be able to be read by anyone. If this is the case, this is a good sing and means your thoughts are clear. What's more, by being both accurate and generous with the description of a sequence, you'll probably use it to recover stage directions, or even dialogue.

The endings table

Creating a table is specific to interactive stories. This table contains all the possible endings and the variables that lead to each branch. In plain language, you count the points.

How many beers does your character have to drink to cause a car accident?

0 – he brakes in time; 1 – he misses the car; 2 – he crashes but no one gets injured; 3 – he crashes and suffers serious injury. At what point can the variable evolve positively (to the bar) or negatively (he takes a nap or eats)?

Revisions – notes

When you rework a sequence, you stroll from mistake to mistake and often forget the reason why you reread the sequence. You need to be careful with this method because with an interactive scenario, this can be dangerous. If you wish to rework a part, don't let yourself get distracted by a new problem. Make note of the mistake you noticed, but finish what you started. A "Revisions" document will be a valuable ally.

An interactive scenario can give you a sense of vertigo. The more the story offers an open universe, the more mistakes manifest themselves. Be methodical in order to resolve them.

The pitch deck

This part can be read at any time and is primarily inspired by what can be done in the audiovisual, radio and video game environments. So, this is a good source of inspiration, right?

Your project's pitch deck should become your best friend. Regardless of what work phase you're in, don't hesitate to add to it whenever an idea or path appears. It's an often laborious process, but it so happens that we write more decks than stories. Indeed, a project is the junction of your desire, a producer's editorial policy and the public's reception. Financing your project means ensuring its artistic and economic viability. Your first mission: seduce! Each project has different needs; it's up to you to highlight your strengths.

The deck consists of several key elements you've heard a thousand times. As part of an interactive scenario, there are, however, some small differences:

- **The short summary (or *pitch*)**. This summary, consisting of a few lines, needs to grab your reader's attention. It has to contain elements such as the setting, the main character and the trigger event. It can also introduce the type of *gameplay*, the replayability and the proposed challenge (if any)[5].

- **The synopsis (one page).** You've succeeded in appealing to your reader with your introduction. From this point, he's looking over your synopsis for twists and turns. This is the occasion to prove to him that you have dense material and you have a mastery of your subject. In general, you don't reveal the ending in your synopsis. Here, the reader is keen to know the different branches or even the different endings.

- **The statement of intent (one page).** This is often a formidable test. You often read that the statement of intent has to answer two questions: why you want to write a story and how. It's not totally false, but it's not the

....

5. The "Série noire" collection offers pitch ideas on *the* back ᶜᵒᵛᵉʳˢ (some updating is still needed).

most important thing. The most important thing is to appeal to the reader by using a rich, precise vocabulary that will draw him into your story.

Moreover, don't get bogged down multiplying the references. The reader expects a clear point of view and has to be able to feel your energy to defend this project.

In an interactive scenario, you have to justify the relevance of this format. *What unique element is the interactivity going to bring to this story?*

And now it's up to you to decide!

How to prepare your work	
A methodology: –The reservoir: the scenes that are going to bring your story to life! –The step outline: the important plot lines that lead to your endings! –The endings table: don't get lost, prepare your endings! –Revisions and notes: all the little things that make the big projects!	The pitch deck: –The summary (pitch): grab their attention! –The synopsis (one page): lively but concise! –The statement of intent (one page): what does the interactive narrative bring to your project?

If you are interested in the history of an interactive scenario, go to *The interactive scenario, a history of a revamped genre.*
If you want to see or see again how to write a scenario, go to *Interactive story fundamentals.*
If you like getting your hands dirty, go to *The mechanics of interactivity.*

David, can you describe your writing process for us?

David Cage: Generally, I start with a story idea that works well with interaction or with an emotion that might work well with interaction.

At all cost, I avoid disassociating the story from the interactivity. I don't like writing a story and then incorporating the interactivity. Rather, I try to link the two from the start of my thought. I love stories that naturally incorporate the interactivity and where the interactivity is at the heart of the concept.

For example, an investigation is always a fantastic narrative engine for interactivity because, in an investigation, I know who I am. I'm an investigator. I know what I'm going to do: look for clues, interrogate witnesses... We have interactivity because I have several ways of solving the investigation. What's more, will I successfully solve the investigation? The interactivity is incorporated in the initial concept.

I work a lot on what is referred to as interactive engines or narrative engines. This is the idea that a story has a dynamic that naturally gravitates toward interactivity and ramification. It's one of the biggest challenges we face at Quantic Dream: finding the narrative engine in all of our concepts. I generally try to give priority to emotion and what the player feels. The idea is to link interactivity to emotion more than anything else.

What are the writing phases?

One of the methods I've developed over the years is to go from macro to micro. I don't like to write big synopses because I've realized that by thinking on too big of a scale, too many things have the appearance they will work. But when you really start writing, it can lead you in a totally different direction or what seemed cool from a macro point of view simply doesn't work when you try to implement it. At the same time, if you are content to write some scenes and see where that takes you, you're going to lack an global view and your story will go nowhere.

That's why I frequently try to go from macro to micro, to re-inject what I find on a micro level on a macro level and to see the consequences. You have to combine structure and scene implementation.

Do you write in English to start with?

No, I always write in French first. It's my native language, and I do not want to add a layer of complexity by thinking in English. I try to make the process as fluid as possible.

Jean-Luc, how do you organize your writing time? What is your method?

Jean-Luc Cano: From 8:30 a.m. to 5:00 p.m. I'm at my computer, and I write all day long. I organize my time based on my projects. I always have two or three at the same time. In general, I always have a feature film, a video game at the same time, and a small short program series. For example, I know that writing a short program takes me two hours. For a feature film, I have to be totally immersed. I need around three weeks where I write on paper first. I write around 50 to 100 scenes. Everything that comes to mind based on one simple idea. Once I've written enough scenes, I start over and ask myself what story I want to tell in the film. I gradually structure my thoughts. I filter my scenes based on my topic to eventually arrive at where I want to be. And the scenes start to gain meaning.

Thomas, how do you generally organize your writing time?

Thomas Veauclin: Considering the scenario from a global standpoint, I establish the beginning and the ending as soon as possible. Then, I establish the story's other big pillars in the middle. And I gradually fill in the rest. For dialogue, I write in a relatively linear fashion, starting at the beginning and going from there. Sometimes, certain sections eventually change what I had planned next. Even so, nothing is set in stone, and I don't hesitate to assume the choices created as I move forward. I mainly write in the morning and at night.

PART 2

THE INTERACTIVE STORY, A HISTORY OF A REVAMPED GENRE

Like any art, an interactive story is forged gradually from its iterations, its expression and its talents. The interactive story first found refuge in the linear medium of books and text-based games that we believed had been buried by video games.

But the explosion video game scene design brought the medium toward narrative maturity, bringing it closer and closer to cinema to later surpass it with real-time writing about emotional experiences that question your choices.

4. CHOOSE-YOUR-OWN-ADVENTURE BOOKS

RENDEZ-VOUS AU 1

Before going into detail, it's good to remind newcomers what a choose-your-own-adventure (CYOA) book is.

It's an interactive book, in other words a book in which the reader is a character and must make several decisions over the course of the story to arrive at the ending. Consequently, the book isn't read in the typical order, from the first to the last page. First of all, you take on the role of the character, put another way, the author explains to you the context and what *you* can do.

The story is divided into paragraphs, 400 being the most common, and at the end of each paragraph, the hero faces different choices. And *you* are the one who makes all those choices. Outside the book itself, you at least need a pencil and eraser, and, in most cases, dice for the fighting. In summary, this is the incredible interactive potential that CYOA books offer. We're completely in interactive scriptwriting, even if the authors (one would need to ask them about this subject in detail) perhaps had never heard of interactive scriptwriting. They were writing books, gamebooks it so happens.

When they appeared in libraries, it was a real success, reaching sales in the millions, all things considered. Why yes, we're really talking about books. Remember, in the '80s video games were just getting going, but they were far from being so popular as they are now in our screens everywhere era. Whereas, nowadays, you can play an impressive number of *roleplaying* video games, back then you had roleplaying games and CYOA books. Addicts would often consume both. The addiction was strong, as strong as it can be with a recreation that develops your taste as it can for reading and the imaginary.

At this point, you ought to situate the subject more or less. So, we'll go over the history a little. If we do some game archeology, the very first gamebook could be *Consider the consequences*, with its evocative title, written by Doris Webster and Mary Alden Hopkins and published in 1930 by The Century Company, in New York. The book lets the reader decide the direction of the story, the interactivity is still limited, there are no characteristics, skills or even any fighting – a very frequent element in most gamebooks.

Nevertheless, one must highlight this effort of literary research, perhaps drawing a connections with a type of literature that represents the era, the crime novel. At the beginning, it was often conceived as a game novel, as the reader was encouraged to discover who was guilty and the author tried to cover the tracks all the while placing evidence. The years between the two world wars is era were the whodunit novel really triumphed. In the shadow of literary glory, the crime novel would eventually be suffer a remarkable upheaval with the appearance of the noir novel, the father of which is none other than Dashiel Hammet and his private detective, Sam Spade. To speak of crime literature is entirely related to our subject, since the art of the story is often studied through the lens of the crime film, a genre of film where the rigor and construction quality lend themselves very well to scriptwriting. And the crime film loves literary adaptation. Since then, you know very well, crime literature has evolved in numerous, prolific directions.

For interactive scriptwriting, after this attempt, one must await new literary explorations such as those of Raymond Queneau in his little *Conte à votre façon* [A Story as You Like it] or his *A Hundred Thousand Billion Poems*, according to which this is the theoretical number of possible combinations according to the author. We must highlight that he founded the Ouvroir de Littérature Potentiel [The Potential Literature Workshop], the Oulipo, with François Le Lionnais, a mathematician and chemist.

It's important to point out these two men's need to combine humanitarian sciences with exact sciences to offer research possibilities. For, what is Oulipo but a literary game? And when you talk about games you talk about rules, and the mathematization of said rules. A video game is simply a universe, no more no less, a game, produced by ever more powerful digital tools.

Interactive scriptwriting is feeling its way, searching for itself, but it still isn't all there yet. Developments in digital technology are not enough for interactive scriptwriting to flourish. The imagination needs to develop still, a fun imagination where one has the desire to go and play, just as one would wish to be transported into a video game. But let's come back to our gamebooks. Their own history is not linked to the original gamebook that presumably gave rise to all the others. No. It was born of a strange red box released on the other side of the Atlantic.

DUNGEONS AND DRAGONS, THE IMAGINARY BOX

It was in 1974 that Gygax and Dave Arneson published this UFO that still shines on in the firmament of the recreational activities of interactive scriptwriting: *Dungeons and Dragons (D&D)*.

Nothing is born by chance, and we will stop playing with Russian nesting dolls by briefly explaining the context in which the famous D&D appeared.

The Lord of the Rings, with the Peter Jackson films, has revamped and validated the planetary success of novels. Indeed, J.R.R. Tolkien's works experienced a resounding post-war success in Britain and America. There was power imaginary material, Tolkien having fully succeeded in writing a text he intended to use to create a myth.

At the same time, after World War Two, *wargames* began to appear. We're still far from *Napoleon Total War*, but it is interesting to see how the development of wargames brings about the need for statistics, simulations and mathematical models.

And here are our *D&D* creators, who have fun fighting with figurines, building them a universe, allowing them to develop from fight to fight, giving them a past... In brief, little by little, a universe appears, characters come to life, and they gradually build a history with each conflict they overcome. What is this but the foundation of a story?

The players, and we're really talking about male players because the vast majority of the people who play are male, play their story to the fullest, they live this story because they play their characters even if, at first glance, it's by means of figurines. However, as their universe gradually takes form, the need for rules arises, for, and this is one of the first necessities of any story, you have to know the possibilities and the limits of the characters.

Without going into detail about what roleplaying games are, here you have some people who get together, who play roles under the auspices of another person who tells them a story and says to them quite often: "And now what do you do?"

Here we are in total interactivity, and the gamemaster, the Dungeon Master, awaits the decisions of the players, submits their actions to some probabilities of success, and adapts his story based on the consequences. Given the impressive scope of the possibilities, first the universe is limited to the area to be explored and the treasure to be discovered, generally by defeating the monster guarding it, if we want to avoid calling it the "boss" at the end of the level.

Do we not find the phases of a scripted video game: the mission briefing, the exploration (in the strict sense), the conflict, the reward. All in an order that can be linear (you advance in the labyrinth) or not (where do you enter the castle? The door, the walls, moats?).

Thus, we can already affirm that the first players, and inevitably the first *Dungeons and Dragons* gamemasters were doing interactive scriptwriting without knowing it. And it's beautiful homage the series *Stranger Things* (Netflix) renders them by putting this game in the spotlight. What a formidable interactive scriptwriting school roleplaying games are! And what an engine for the imagination. Very few science fiction, fantasy or fantastical writers forty or under, at least in France, did not experience roleplaying games, whether as an amateur or a professional.

It is interesting to note that at the time *Dungeons and Dragons* came out, the first mainstream console video games started to appear (Atari was founded in 1972).

When talking about video games, to give you an idea of the *D&D*'s success and its connection with video games, Tom Selleck, alias Magnum P.I., plays *Dungeons and Dragons* in episode 12 of season 5 (1985).

THE FOUNDING FATHERS

In Europe, the people who created the first gamebooks or CYOA books are also the people who would go on to distribute the very first *D&D* game in Europe:

Steve Jackson and Ian Livingstone. As you know, the first CYOA books were English. When they published *The Warlock of Firetop Mountain* in 1982 as the first "Fighting Fantasy" book, they took a small step forward in the publishing world, but a great leap in the imaginary world. And things got exciting very quickly. Their first book was translated in France in 1983 by Gallimard, as part of the "Folio junior" collection. The first CYOA was heroic fantasy, and it must be remember that this is still the main genre.

French readers were quick to praise this new way of reading, which addressed subjects criticized in so-called general literature. This new literature was idea literature for a young audience and not just any. It was for adolescents. I'll let you figure out the age range that defines adolescence, but it's true that trying to please this damned hypersensitive adolescents is still a headache in the publishing world. The CYOA books immediately won them over and ushered in happy days at Gallimard.

To give you an idea of the magnitude, one book from the "Lone Wolf" series sold 100,000 copies. At Pelican there was even a "Choose Your Own Adventure with Gérard de Villiers" collection! All the excitement led some French readers to pursue writing as a profession, including Doug Headline, a rather Anglo-Saxon pseudonym it's true, the son of Jean-Patrick Manchette, a dearly beloved writer of crime fiction in France. And we've told you that crime literature, by its construction, leads to a story! Given his connections in publishing, Doug Headline, for example, was able to create the "Haute Tension" ["High Voltage"] collection at Hachette that brought together a whole team of writers. Other authors, such as Gildas Sagot, also enriched the "Folio Junio" catalog.

An deluge of books, both French and otherwise, inundated bookstores, supermarkets and even libraries and school documentation and information centers, often finding a second life at second-hand book sellers. Available in paperback for quite a reasonable price in francs and illustrated by talented artists such as Russ Nicholson and Gary Chalk, the CYOA books titillated and enriched the imagination of an entire generation. For the people who would search the aisles for a little fun of their own during the family shopping, seeing the "Lone Wolf" or "Défis et Sortilèges" ["Trials and Sorcery"] logo was the promise of a piece of somewhere else and a bit like a dream.

The CYOA genre, both English and French, basically developed in parallel. It's a good thing for a publisher to be able to earn customer loyalty by guaranteeing customers other books, and it's a true pleasure for the reader, who can discover another parcel of these marvelous worlds, often by following the hero's adventures, even developing his abilities, making him more and more likely to succeed at his missions. It must noted that the "Fighting Fantasy" series, with the sword and shield logo, never offered to develop a hero. It is always about an adventure in the same universe, that of Titan, with rare exceptions such as the very "mad-maxian" *Combattant de l'autoroute* (Freeway Fighter). Sometimes, one could find a connection between two stories, like with *Return to Firetop Mountain* in 1992, but playing a previous adventure didn't have any direct effect. However, many authors discovered the interest of playing a recurring character who gradually gains experience from story to story. In this category, and this is what made it successful, the "Lone Wolf" series by Joe Dever won people over with its hero, who mastered new skills in a world endowed with a storyline spread over several books. Few are the CYOA players who have never faced the Dark Masters.

The number of books rapidly increased, and soon one could play elsewhere just as easily as in a fantasy universe, like in *le Mercenaire de l'espace* (The Space Mercenary), from 1985. Historical series appeared, such as the "History" series by "Folio junior," as CYOA books lent themselves to historical fiction with an added little pedagogical bonus. Literary characters were also used, such as the famous Sherlock Holmes, in the series of the same name by "Folio junior." In the other literary genres, publishers drew on a wide range of superheros (*Superpouvoirs* (Superpowers) by Haute tension), bloodcurdling horror (*les Portes Interdites* (Forbidden Gates), also by Gallimard), and a little science fiction (*Car Wars*, by Haute tension). The last of these remains the least represented. This is interesting because the 1980s, for many people, would be a turning point, not to mention a decline, in science fiction literature. I assure you, the debate on this subject is still far from over. CYOAs drew on myth in the tragic series "Chroniques crétoises" ("Cretian Chronicles"), Homeric as can be, and broadened the horizons of many readers by taking inspiration from a good many then largely unknown civilizations, such as in Asia. Who didn't want to become a ninja, well before *Naruto*, after reading *Way of the Tiger*? There were even humorours series and genre parodies, such as those by the talented J.H. Brennan. If you've never read Excalibur Junior, you don't know the Arthurian universe!

The modes of storytelling and interactivity grew richer and more developed. It became possible to play as several characters, two or more, depending on the series. In this sense, the series "Double jeu" ("Double game") has an evocative name. Borrowing from roleplaying games and the adventures offered to the players, it is possible to find series to play by yourself in a roleplaying game universe, like in "Œil Noir" ("Black Eye"). The series "L'Épée de légende" ("Blood Sword"), allows you to play a whole team in the "Terres de légendes" ("Dragon Warriors") universe, which, translated to French, is an excellent roleplaying game for sale in paperback. The RPG *Fighting Fantasy* was published soon after but wasn't translated until decades later.

CYOA authors have always push the boundaries of interactivity and the richness of the universes offered. Consequently, you can guess what ultimately brought them down: computer and console games. The onslaught of electronic games in the 1990s, simply put, swept aside youth books, which at the time offer inferior interactivity and offered outdated visuals. And yet, it's incredible how a few paragraphs stringing together fights and riddles really stirred the imagination. The black and white illustrations were the ultimate springboard that propelled the reader into another world and time.

In the 1990s, there was a lot of nostalgia. While one series after another came to an end, publishers and authors fought to keep the genre alive. The big series like "Fighting Fantasy" and "Lone Wolf" stagnated. New publishers interested in CYOAs, often small enterprises, looked to offer a little something else. Who remembers Yeti ? The fight for survival for publishers worsened.

NEW ACTORS FOR A NEW CHALLENGE

The Internet has allowed a small community of fans to make links and propose adventures online, since, as it happens, hypertext links work exactly like a CYOA. On the web you'll find Rendez-vous au 1 (http://rdv1.dnsalias.net/forum/), fightingfantasy.com or even litteraction.fr. And there's also the French CYOA database, Planete LDVEH (http://planete-ldvelh.com/).

In France, one can date this renewed passion for CYOAs to the partnership between Gallimard and Le Grimoire. It's through video games that the CYOA book made a comeback... thanks to a roleplaying game based on one of the most well-known series, the famous "Lone Wolf" by Joe Dever and Gary Chalk. The English publisher, Mongoose Publishing, released the *Lonewolf* roleplaying game in 2004, and Le Grimoire released an updated and expanded version in French in 2007. This was the very first translation supplemented by the fans. However, the consulting work had begun at Gallimard, which re-edited at least the first twenty volumes of the "Lone Wolf" series in 2006, then "Fighting Fantasy" in 2007, in the format we have already mentioned.

This resurgence is not a tidal wave, it has nothing to do, for example, with the wave of manga and the emblematic ninja, Naruto, which was capable of representing up to 14% of manga sales alone from 2007 to 2011.

But when Gallimard publishes some previously unreleased "Fighting Fantasy" again, it was another sign, starting with *L'œil d'émeraude* (The Emerald Eye) in 2007, an almost mythical book among fans that had yet to be translated.

Here we have to distinct approaches between Gallimard and Hachette, one more creative, the other based on technical specifications. If, like with Sherlock Holmes, the idea of using a well-known literary character isn't new in the CYOA world, the idea of product licensing seems more recent to us. "Custom adventures" at Hachette have only been around since 2011, but they are based on *Star Wars*, *Prince of Persia*, etc. Note that this is a comparison, not a critique.

While big publishing houses are beginning to reoccupy the landscape and small publishers are clearing the way and exploring new directions, we can affirm in 2018 that choose-your-own-adventure books continue to delight their audience.

PRO INSIGHT

Erwan, how do you come to interactive storytelling?

Erwan Le Breton: I discovered interactive storytelling with *The Warlock of Firetop Mountain*, by Steve Jackson and Ian Livingstone, which was the first book where you're the hero I ever read. I bought it because it was in the paperback section next to the Sci-Fi or fantasy novels would devour at the time.

.The cover said, "Dice required, this is a book you play." Okay. And leafing through it, I saw "end of paragraph, you can now do this or that, and then go to such page." I immediately loved it. I said to myself: "This really is the book where I'm the hero, I decide what happens!"

So, now that I'm a "veteran" of interactive fiction, I'm well aware that these choices are situated in a confined, pre-determined framework, but it still gave that same thrilling feeling of "my story's not the same as my brother's, even though he read the same book."

This is precisely what distinguishes interactive fiction from other forms of storytelling. That feeling we call *agency* in English. More than true freedom, or choice, it's the actually the impression that you have an impact. The possibility to say to yourself "It's me who's in charge, I'm in control of what happens, I decide where I go."

When you see a film, when you watch a TV series, when you read a book, you sit in the passenger's seat, and you let the driver take you where he feels like taking you. Sometimes, you know where you're going, sometimes it's a surprise, but you're not continually telling him "Here, I'd like you to change direction, or stop, or go faster," whereas with interactivity, you actually do this, you change direction, speed, rhythm. You really have the feeling you're in control.

There is often a debate about "more control for the player/reader = less artistic control, thus less narrative quality, less meaning, less richness, less emotional impact." I think that there are some interactive works now that leave you, when you finish them, a real feeling of accomplishment, of memories, an emotional residue, you know, something strong. On the other hand, there are some linear works, and there always have been some, that leave you indifferent, which don't manage to produce this little bit of magic. So, it has more to do with the quality of the writing, and also how the context and the characters relate to your own feelings, as opposed to the fact that it's very scripted, very linear or very interactive with lots of *player agency*.

5. TEXT-BASED GAMES AND NARRATIVE-BASED VIDEO GAMES

TO START, A BIT OF FANTASY!

In a hole lived a hobbit... In fantasy, and at the heart of the universe of the most famous roleplaying game, *Dungeons and Dragons*, the universe of J.R.R. Tolkien is essential. And it incontestably was for the first text-based game in video game history, which was created by William Crowther in 1976. As he himself states in *Genesis II, Creation and Recreation with Computers*, by Dale Peterson, published in 1983, William Crowther played *Dungeons and Dragons* and also explored caves; it's not a far stretch to say that this predestined him, joyfully enough, to write subterranean adventures.

Consequently, when he started to write the first text-based game, initially for his children, he found inspiration in roleplaying games and his own knowledge of speleology, and wrote *Adventure*, which would later become *Colossal Cave Adventure*, originally inspired by Mammoth Cave (without mammoths, however) in Kentucky (United States). A game whose translation to French we owe to Jean-Luc Pontico, which you can download for free (the translated game, not Jean-Luc Pontico).

ADVENTURE AT YOUR FINGERTIPS

William Crowther explains that he wanted a game that non-computer people could play (already!), and, above all, no requirements except knowing how to type in English on a keyboard. Initially programmed using FORTRAN, *Adventure* allows the male player (at the time, let's be clear, there were not female players) to use a natural language based on the actions he wants to take, using a syntax analyzer. This generally consists of a verb, and you have to use the right one, plus an object or a place, etc. Very often, to move, you just have to click on the desired direction. The first text-based game really only has text. You only move using text, you only act using text, and the game only gives you information using text. What's more, during your first game, it often tells you it doesn't understand what you want...

It inevitably has bugs, just like every other video game ever created obviously; Don Woods, a colleague of the creator, debugged and expanded it. Here, we touch on one of the fundamental notions of text-based video games, which they with roleplaying games: sharing and exchanging. Indeed, anyone who wants to develop the game can do it, which also poses difficulties in finding the original game file. Naturally, if you play *Colossal Cave Adventure*, often simply referred to as *Adventure*, you're in the original story if the maximum score is 350 points. However, this score is, it appears, virtually impossible to reach. Indeed, everything depends on the game's creator, thus the ease of the riddles, the difficulty of the tests, etc., rely on the player's imagination. And you need to use your imagination when all you have is a line or two of text – it's not chapters of novels. The text is basically informative in nature, although this doesn't exclude a small effort at pleasantries. If you don't take any notes, orienting yourself gets complicated really quickly because you don't advance in a straight line. Thus, heading westward doesn't mean "if you retrace your steps, you head back east" – in the meantime you went down a fork in the road, turned, etc. However, all you have is text, and you can quickly get angry once you're well and truly lost.

Like in roleplaying games, and in choose-your-own-adventure books, you find treasure, you search sites, you face creatures and tests. Fantasy is at the heart of creating and developing interactive narrative, regardless of the medium.

TEXT-BASED GAMES TAKE OFF!

Other text-based games would come, and the most famous of them would be *Zork*, by Infocom, which appeared in 1980, after a good four years in development. To put things in context, these games were sold in boxes at the time. The Web didn't exist (as opposed to the Internet, i.e. Arpanet as Crowther was working on his game), so you needed to own a micro-computer... The difficulty for game makers was to get outside the university environment and sell it to other people besides the creators and beta testers.

At the same time, very soon after, the forerunner to the MMORPG was released. MUD, which stands for *Multi-User Dungeon*, appeared in 1978, thanks to Roy Trubshaw and Richard Bartle. Thus, they created what would be the first MUD. Once again, the reference to *Dungeons and Dragons* is clear, and MUD borrows techniques from the text-based game *Adventure*. Obviously, in 1978, things are a lot less connected than with *World of Warcraft*... MUDs retain a cooperative and collaborative spirit; you can, if you know how to program a little in any case, give yourself a portion of the game and develop it.

Over a ten-year period, from 1976 to 1986, text-based adventure games would develop further, switch to color and include images. Text-based games are quite light, even as *Zork* grew in size over its many versions, it was never any bigger than a megabyte. And yes, a three and quarter inch floppy disk, for those of you've used floppy disks, wasn't nothing. Infocom, the company that created *Zork*, presumably sold a million copies. That gives you an idea of the players' interest in this type of adventure. "Big Bang Theory," a series that started in 2006 and now in its 11[th]season in2017 (note the logic), regularly makes reference to *Zork*.

These creations were for the most part Anglo-Saxon. *The Hobbit* (What did we tell you?), by Austrian developers Beam Software, was a hit in 1982. In France, we can highlight Froggy Software, hooray, or rather "ribbit! ribbit!" But like froggy, text-based adventure games would soon take a plunge.

BETTER TO DIE THAN DISAPPEAR!

It's easy to understand what's going to kill the passion for these games: the development of video games themselves, which would become more and more beautiful, yes, even in the era of the triumphant pixel. Point and click (P&C) games would eventually prevail: no more need to type "search cave," or think of the right verb, read a few lines or imagine what you see or what you need to do. From this point on, you explore directly with your mouse's arrow. We note, however, that these P&C games were still interactive stories. It's the game design that changed, and not just a little...

As you read in the part about choose-your-own-adventure books, they were threated with extinction but resisted and began to revamp the genre. It was the same for text-based games, which teetered on the verge of oblivion. And with computers, as with literature, it's all a matter of language.

Brit Graham Nelson created Inform to develop Z-machine games, allowing them develop them like Infocom (the creator of *Zork*). And what media did the game developers turn to for inspiration in this language? Choose-your-own-adventure books. You can see it. The uroboros rejoices. The snake well and truly bites its own tail, much to the delight of the players. Yes, we're in the 1990s. We'll resume our bias, even if in this decade the players are still mostly male.

There are even some "players' rights," in 17 articles, to limit the game creator's omnipotence with respect to the player's blindness, limited to the text alone and often dependent on the turn of a phrase. We note that we find this game notion, in terms of narrative, and rights, quite frequently in literature. Indeed, in 1928 S.S. Van Dine, crime novel author, published 20 rules for crime fiction authors in *American Magazine*, not without a certain irony, to indicate what should no longer be done in a crime novel considered to be a gamebook: the reader must have a chance to figure out who did it. Previously, we talked about Oulipo in France and its taste for games and creation, and if we remain within France, how can we not think of the readers' rights written by Daniel Pennac?

The history of text-based adventure games might have gone no further, limited to a community of geeks.

A GAME RESURGENCE!

Smart phones and digital tablets are going to bring a breath of fresh air and, above all, new visibility to text-based adventure games, which are totally becoming narrative-based video games. And they aren't just being made in English speaking countries now, but also in France.

The text is always present, but it's not alone. The quite recent success (2015) of *Lifeline* is emblematic: use a light, easy-to-implement technology in an application, and suddenly you're launching into space on a rescue mission! Note that a syntax analyzer is not longer needed; nowadays, you choose from the actions/responses offered to you, like in choose-your-own-adventure books. Here, if we're unable to reconcile the reading and the video game – the book the object and the activity digital – then there isn't much more we can do!

This is all the more true now that software such as Twin (this book will talk about this more in detail) all anybody and everybody to build their own interactive adventures – we're getting a little ahead of ourselves, but if you've never written an interactive story, to get a quick and easy rundown, Twine is worth a look around. And what year was Twine created in? In 2007, the same year as the iPhone. It's enough to make you think there's some kind of conspiracy. Twine's creator, Chris Klimas, deserves his place in the interactive storywriting hall of fame.

Yes, there's other software out there, but this is a book; he's not aiming for exhaustiveness, and we like Twine a lot. Since then, however, other software such as Celestory Creator (we'll talk more about this too) have brought things to a new level. The future of interactive storywriting has only just begun, if we may go so far to say.

As for the mainstream, there are increasingly more story-driven video games, in the image of the "Grand Theft Auto" series or the "God of War" games.

However, it was in the early 2010s that purely narrative-based games, born from the *point & click* tradition (games with quests and riddles to solve on the screen) shifted towards a new style of playability: morality.

The emotion takes quite a particular place, and the enjoyment is the constant anticipation of the consequences of these choices on the story, which begins to sprawl. This narrative exploration becomes a real challenge for games acclaimed by both fans and critics (BAFTA for best story for *Heavy Rain* in 2010 and for *The Walking Dead* in 2013, respectively selling 5 and 30 millions copies, *The Walking Dead* being, at the time of release, less expensive and available on many gaming platforms), as it gives there studios a reputation for an all new approach to storytelling in video games, the challenge of which is to continually renew the formula.

In 2018, the interactive story-based game market can be divided into several categories:

- Independent stand-alone video games, in other words, games thought to have a life all their own. We often find a chatbot style format (sms simulation). Each project is a challenge, and the success of sequels is not guaranteed.
- Interactive storytelling platforms based on large quantities of productions and strong user retention, *via* credit purchasing or subscription The

concept of serialization is fully utilized. The common format is *visual novels* (comic books where you are the hero).

- Stand-alone PC/console games in 3D that one could classify as AA or AAA based on their ambition. The staging is very advanced and cinematographic and sometimes involves motion capture (which captures the 3D movements of real actors). These projects are very costly, take months, even several years, to develop, and are particularly risky. Technical mastery is essential and costly.

Benjamin, what does triple A qualityimply?

Benjamin Diebling : A great number of choices and quality graphics. At Quantic Dream, we work on realism because this creates empathy vis-à-vis the story. Realism gives the impression that you're in a true story, were every is real, where the characters look real.

We push the quality of the graphics of course, but there's something else: the number of choices, and their consequences. Each choice has a consequence, and each player will have their story and the subsequent consequences. The most important thing, however, is the story. Each choice is real, and you can feel it in your decisions. Everything goes from there. I would say that graphics and the cinematographic tools serve the story, rather.

What are the big production phases of a triple A game?

You write the game's statement of intent, what the game is going to look like. Then, you begin making the scenery, the characters, every little thing you're going to see. You need to be flexible and adaptable, and there are changes, several versions. Sometimes scenes disappear, etc. Things get canceled. It happens. On the other hand, you have to have the best story possible.

Can you talk to us a little about the production of a story-based 3D game?

For the production, you write, you conceptualize, in other words you draw on *concept art*, you do camera testing to see the format, and to see what the game is going to look like cinematically, too. We give try it, it works, we can also change over the course of production. Sometimes, it's positive to make changes. Production doesn't really exist as such. There isn't a magic recipe, method or technique as opposed to cinema. Each studio has its own process and method based on its games. It's all about understanding the studio and its process so that things work.

What are your references in interactive storytelling and why?

Sybil Collas: I've very fond of games that nourish their story with their *gameplay* and their narrative design, such as *Brothers: A Tale of Two Sons, Life is Strange, Paper Please, Her Story, Reigns, Undertale, Monument Valley, A Normal Lost Phone, Lifeline, Florence, Frostpunk*, etc. Games by *That Game Company*, Alexis Kennedy or Xalavier Nelson Jr. always impact the player. Their way of telling a story is so subtle that it's hard to immediately identify it. Most of the time, the games that leave a deep, lasting impact are games that use less text and put more focus on *gameplay* that makes sense, on the impact on the player, on the character's evolution, or on how the story is told through the environment. The choices are not the only way to build a narrative around the player: the gameplay and the challenge/reward layout, regardless of the form it takes, are powerful narrative instruments.

If we talk about games with impactful storytelling and/or strong writing, we can include most, if not all, of the games by Double Fine and Tim Schafer, games by interactive fiction makers *Choice of Games*, intellectual properties such as *The Wolf Among Us*, the series *The Blackwell Legacy*, the games *The Last of Us, The Stanley Parable, Transistor, Tales from the Borderlands, Bioshock, Portal*, or even more modest games like *Hungry Hearts Dinner, Doki Doki Literature Club*, or *Analogue: A Hate Story*. You'll note that there are still a lot of other games, from independent to triple A, that have excellent content and a lot to teach us – the games cited are just the ones I prefer and am able to fit into my response.

Joe Pinney: *Walking Dead season 1* is really special for me. This game showed me the power of interactive storytelling. I didn't just identify with the lead character and his relationships, I was the lead character, and the relationships were mine. I cried at the end, even though I was involved in the game development and knew what was going to happen.

FibreTigre: It's hard not to cite Steve Jackson (the English one). *The Craft of Adventure* by Graham Nelson, available for free on the Internet and written in 1995 is also a reference I detail in my IF courses.

Thomas Veauclin: *Planescape Torment, Myst* and *Riven, The Stanley Parable* but also films like *Memento, Angel Heart, Crash* or even *7 Pounds*.

PART 3

INTERACTIVE STORY FUNDAMENTALS

An art is conveyable based on the codes of the results of the experiences that witnessed its creation. You need to know them, even if your goal is to liberate yourself from them.

From genre to the dialogue, including the hero and the cast of characters, mastering these fundamentals will help you get a handle of the situation more quickly, avoid traps, innovate and give a framework to the life of your interactive narrative.

6. SCENARIO ARCHITECTURE

INTRODUCTION TO SCRIPTWRITING: STRUCTURE

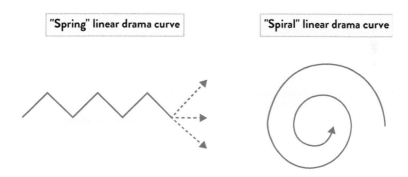

"Spring" linear drama curve

"Spiral" linear drama curve

The first graph (left) shows a structure based on the spring principle. The resolution of each scene is positive or negative. When you place the spectator under pressure, you press down on the spring. On the other hand, it's important to know when to reduce the pressure in order to create an emotional elevator. The objective is simple: maintain (by alternating) the player's attention.

The second graph, in the shape of spiral, is used for tragedy. The destiny of the main character is contained within. He cannot escape his fate. Any attempt inevitably brings him back on the path leading to his destiny.

Writing an interactive story involves a first necessity: the desire to write.

Next, you'll have to apply a particular form of willpower known as discipline. Without rules for writing, you'll inevitably develop an interactive story that goes in all directions, and your fragmented story will go nowhere.

Consequently, ask yourself this very good question: do you really want to write an interactive story? Is it so you can eat and earn a living? Very well, but you're advised, then, to make an interactive story with limited ambitions so as to better grasp the techniques and difficulties specific to this type of writing. Want to write the work of your life? Think carefully, does it need an interactive story? For, by choosing to write an interactive story, the story you carry inside you, the story you want to tell the world, may take a long time to write. Do you enjoy writing page after page, plunging into your universe, and choosing witty retorts for your characters? You have to be convinced of one thing, writing an interactive story is hard work and discouraging.

You've been warned. If you close this book, go to the cover. Otherwise, continue on.

So, you have a desire to write. Writing an interactive story means writing a game, and with a game you need mechanics. And with mechanics, you have to develop them, test them and put them together piece by piece. To make your interactive story purr like a formula 1 car in pole position, you have to fine tune it in the garage. Don't hesitate to tighten a nut here, a bolt there. And when a part doesn't work, you have to set it aside and never force it.

You really have to be conscious of the notion of working in stages. Not that you have to apply writing methods like a laboratory technician. There's nothing worse, and it's surest method to write nothing. But you can't write your interactive story in one go, as soon as an idea comes to you.

If you write short stories, novels, forget about this immersion. If you normally write stories, you already have a notion of stages. And if you are working in video games, which is likely, you'll be convinced of it.

This matters a lot to the mechanical aspect of the game, however, it's especially important, fundamentally, to the story, to the stories. If you think of several endings, it's, well, quite obvious: you cannot write all the stories leading to them at the same time. Like a centipede, your story must advance with rigor, so that, for the player – and for everyone who's going to work on it – everything flows by itself, without the player even noticing the changes in direction, without getting confused.

Think of it this way: without your interactive story, there won't be a game. You're the one who's going to make everything possible; without you, the ideas, the universe, all the things the humans bring to them, the things they exchange, the things they dream of, will never come to fruition. Everyone has ideas, but if you basically take the intellectual property code, the person who writes the story is the author, even if he's not the one who had the idea or came up with the topic. The idea of a croissant is only an idea until the baker has taken it out of the oven. This may seem obvious to you, but remember it when it's necessary. Because this story, as you will see, won't write itself, or without effort.

You're the one who's going to write the story, and you may share the task with several others, but without you to write the story, there won't be anything. Without you to mold the essential clay that is the imagination, there will be no one to repel the nothingness.

So, are you pumped up? Let's get started them!

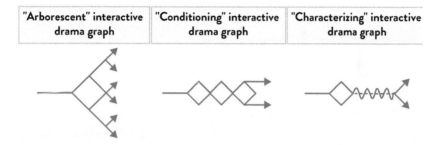

"Arborescent" interactive drama graph	"Conditioning" interactive drama graph	"Characterizing" interactive drama graph

The first graph shows the most complex interactive form. Indeed, the player's choices have consequences and cause a snowball effect. This structure relies on points of no return the effects of which the player must feel in her adventure. The desire for replayability is complete. The interactive promise is kept.

The second graph shows a more modest arborescence in terms of work and, thus, production time. Certain choices (big ones) are conditioned, and thus certain sequences are not accessible. Replayability is partial. The goal is to find a good balance to maintain the illusion as long as possible.

Lastly, the third graph shows the most economical form. The choices of action don't have real consequences. On the other hand, a lot of characterization work is done. The dialogue choices allow the player to build her own main character profile. The secondary characters are the center of this structure. The desire for replayability is weak. However, the experience may be entirely personalized by focusing on the dialogue writing.

David, what would be your advice to a young interactive story author?

David Cage: It's hard to give advice, but I would say... Be crazy. Don't try to recreate a game you like, or games that were made thirty years ago. You need to pay attention to the medium. What new ideas are you going to bring? Naturally, it's useful to take inspiration from old games, but you have to offer something new at the same time.

Sometimes, some authors are timid and don't trust their instinct or simply aren't bold enough. They tell themselves: "This idea is great, but it's too twisted for a studio to be interested..." Being unique is never a problem, it's a strength. That's why people will want to work with you. Being unique is an incredible challenge because, when you're different, you come up against a lot of resistance. People will tell you that it'll never work, that it's never been done before... And that's exactly why it's a brilliant idea.

Be brave, be crazy, follow your instinct, don't listen to people who say you can't do it because everyone will say that. Have faith in what you believe and try to do something that makes sense. Sometimes, it's better to fail with something you are proud of rather than succeeding with something you're ashamed of.

Sybil, do you have any advice for authors wishing to get a start in writing interactive stories?

Sybil Collas: Finish what you start and share your work. An unfinished work, however great, cannot be test or appropriately read – and keeping your work to yourself doesn't do anyone any good except for your ego. Creative work means failing, again and again. You have to learn to embrace your failures and understand the benefit there is to failing. Think of failure as a friend. Search it out. Fail, you're being given the chance to try. Ask for feedback, learn from your mistakes, detach yourself from your creations, destroy them, remake them! Nothing you do will be perfect, ever. But it will be better. Beware of impostor syndrome and negative stress. There will be abyss between what you are and what you dream of being. But don't let that bother. Establish some small, hard-to-avoid progress markers and take the time to identify and celebrate the points, however so small, you succeeded at improving from one project to another. And read *Creativity Inc.* by Edwin Catmull, and *On Writing* by Stephen King.

Erwan, do you have any advice for future video game scriptwriters?

Erwan Le Breton: First, and this is an essential piece of advice, even if you don't have a publisher, write something "visible." This can be periodic blog, it can be a web comic if you find an illustrator, a web series with a director, this can be a self-published book, not necessarily a novel, this can be a collection of short stories, or even a choose-your-own adventure book.

Basically, finish a writing project and don't be content to just accumulate story ideas, synopsis drafts or first chapters in a drawer. The idea is to be able to show something when you have an interview and be able to say, "Look what I made."

One tip: even if it requires some money, participate in writing workshops. There are few in France compared to English-speaking countries, but they're coming along. It's often a little expensive, but it's worth it.

And then, last point, it's good to bear in mind that you will rarely be working alone. If your mindset is "It's *my* artistic vision," it's not going to be easy. Even for a comic book, you have to integrate the illustrator's style and opinions. For a video game, you have to at least add a game designer, sound director, art director, perhaps some other writers, etc. In sum, it's a collaborative work. So, that means working for the project, accepting critiques, being flexible, accepting changes, redos, and not coming into work saying, "it's my way or the highway."

Your role is going to be to participate in the creation, to enhance it, to bind it together, but don't except the development team to make the interactive version of your novel – unless we're talking about a very well-known author and that's the deal.

Joe, any advice for authors wanting to get a start in writing interactive stories?

Joe Pinney: First, take a leap and create something! The tools are there. Build something very small over the time you have available. Share it with friends, share it online, get commentary. Then, build something else. There's no better way to learn.

Secondly, get in touch with people who do what you want to do. If you want a job at a video game company, find people at that company who will talk with you. Ask for advice, politely. Stay in touch, politely. Over time, you'll find a way in.

Thirdly, persevere. Creative work is an emotional roller coaster. It's hard to complete and share your work. It's hard to accept critiques. It's difficult when projects are canceled, which is unfortunately very common in the entertainment industry. Love your work, learn to roll with the punches and keep going.

FibreTigre, do you have any advice for authors wanting to get a start in writing interactive stories?

FibreTigre: You have to read the classics. *Sorcery, Creature From Havoc,* or even just *The Warlock from Firetop Mountain...* This will save you years of trying to perfect yourself if you understand the genius of these works.

A SOLID FOUNDATION: A UNIVERSE AND ITS CHARACTERS

Depending on the story you want to write, things aren't necessarily made in order. You may perhaps first have a very strong idea about your main character, or you may have an magnificent idea about a completely new world and what might very well happen there. Things are going to evolve in your mind at the same time, not to mention the secondary characters. So long as the foundation of your story hasn't been written out word for word, one of your secondary characters could even taken on an unexpected importance at the beginning.

As you can understand, we're offering you different points to follow in a logical order that may be different from the order in which you create things, but in any case, you will pass through these points because, without them, there is no story. Obviously, you can get experimental, but by definition, it's up to you to take the risks, so it's hard for us to tell you how do that in this book.

If you want take a look at universe creation, go to *Creating a universe and mastering its codes.*

If you want to take a look at how main character is born, go to *Main character.*

If you prefer to fill out your secondary characters, go to *The cast of secondary characters.*

As for the universe and the characters, we will not make distinctions about the media you decide to work with for your interactive story. In any case, you need a universe and characters, and there isn't really a difference in creating it all depending on the media. True, a purely visual universe would be uninteresting for an audio-only game, but we assume you have a minimum of good sense.

7. CREATING A UNIVERSE AND MASTERING ITS CODES

A story inevitably takes place somewhere (and this somewhere could well be understood as plural), and if take places nowhere, it is already a universe.

Obviously, you are the creator, so you create the universe you want for your story.

We already brought up this subject at the start of the book, but it's time to ask you about genres. Indeed, the power and the inconvenience of a genre is that it offers you a universe with pre-established codes.

AND HERE, WE'LL THINK ABOUT GENRES

What to choose: science fiction, crime, erotic, horror?

Choosing a genre doesn't give you a precise universe, it gives you codes. If you opt for the crime genre, we expect a contemporary story, in our world. It's up to you to choose the country/countries, the crime(s), etc. But in theory, there are no extraterrestrials or magical formulas. The world must remain rational, or at least explainable with what we know of our own reality nowadays, let's say. In a crime story, if there isn't one investigator, we expect to find the opposite, such as gangsters, serial killers, etc. If you choses these options here, then your codes are going to evolve. With a serial killer, one expects ritualized killings, with gangsters, paybacks or the rise or fall of a character, etc.

It's an increasingly accepted fact: you can cross genres.

If you situate your crime story in the 19th century, you're crossing the crime and historical fiction genres. If you situate it in the century after your era, you're it with science fiction. Then you can add a serial killer and shift it all toward the codes of a horror film, and then... Careful when you mix, hybridize – use the term you like – when you cross genres, it will all be a matter of finding the right formula for the codes and revelations you offer your player. Indeed, you can either tell your player from the start that it's a medieval, horror, sci-fi universe or you can plan some twists to shake the universe, once, twice, etc. And here, a twist isn't easy at all. It relies on the element of surprise, even if only a partial surprise, and you need to make it a good one, not a bad one. The player has to say to herself, "Cool, zombies!" not "Zombies again..."

For now, what we're interested in with genres are their codes. Do you not know the codes? Do you not know the genres? Then, watch some films, some series, play, etc.

You'll also notice that genres serve as marketing labels, just as a game, a film or a novel becomes a "genre all its own." Over time, *Star Wars*, whether you like, love or hate it, has become a genre all its own. Take Sherlock Holmes, reworked in some many ways. There's either a total respect for the codes (the pipe, the lines, the method, etc.) or there's a play on the codes in someway, but Sherlock Holmes, while in essence one can classify him as crime fiction, has become Sherlock Holmes *the genre*.

True, we can begin debating what is and what isn't a myth, but here we need to be brief about it. Let's cut to the quick by saying that a myth, if one can adapt it, use it and freely transform it, it belongs to common fantasy. In this sense, *Star Wars* is far from being a myth, in spite of its lofty discourse.

As Ray Bradbury said, and certainly plenty of others before him, to your write, you have to cultivate yourself, regardless of your culture. First off, this gives you some ideas, and thus you'll surely see what is often done, too often done or, more rarely, what is never done. This last aspect is a delicate matter, it's always harder to speculate about what isn't there. Do we never talk about this subject because it's culturally taboo, invisible, dangerous, etc.? Actually, sometimes there's a good reason why no one has ever done something in such or such a way: because it doesn't work.

Your genre (or your genres if you're mixing them) is going to allow you to know what your characters can do, and also what you can do to them. And the players will also have an idea of that, even if, and it's often expected, you area able to surprise them: it's your margin of freedom. Genres can be stifling and bland if you use clichés one after another; true, you'll have written a horror, goth or historical fiction story, but it will have no taste. Only the players discovering this type of story for the first time may find it interesting, and from this point of view, that's the power of youth, for marketing, for example.

You must admit that it's a real shame to put together something that resembles a pizza but doesn't even taste like one!

So, yes, it's one thing to take one or two genres, but it's completely another to respect the codes and play with them.

No one ever said making a good story is easy, and if it reassures you, writing a successful story doesn't necessarily involve writing a good story. We're being subjective, and ultimately the numbers will do the talking.

For an interactive story, you're subject to the same constraints, or worse.

Indeed, the interest in choosing a genre is, firstly, to provide you a coherent universe, where the codes available, even if violating the laws of physics, con-tribute to a coherent universe. A player playing sci-fi often expects... normally shouldn't expect anything – if she expects something in particular, it's likely that there sci-fi culture is limited to a given branch of the genre. And that's normal. Not everyone has the time, desire or leisure to fumbling around a genre in all directions. If your player's only reference is *Star Wars*, a universe à la Buster Keaton on Jupiter will be a big surprise to her, and it's hard to say whether it'll be a good or bad surprise, here. Thus, with genres we understand the irritation with certain universes, i.e. licensed universes: you at least know that a given audience is going to like it, so there's a better idea of the profitability. If it's possible to like creating a licensed universe, it all depends on the freedom you are given. Indeed, if nothing corresponds to the universe in question anymore, rejection is likely.

Okay, okay, this doesn't solve your problem, creating a universe base on one or more genres. In fact, it's the same difficulty as creating a universe without a genre (although you very often find a branch to cling to), and the problem is coherence.

Genres offer coherent universes because the codes give the genre body and vice versa. You can play with the DNA of a genre and crossbreed it with others, but the baby has to be viable and, if possible, have several attributes. And this DNA is the codes.

A classic case of manipulating the DNA in excess is parody. You take all the codes and you make a mock of them. Comedy is a genre in its own right and, perhaps, one of the most difficult because the player is going to expect to laugh. Obviously, humor is not to be excluded from you story, but it's a matter of including the right amount, in the desired tone. Here, if you make fun of genre A to Z, you won't have written a genre film, you'll have parodied it.

Conversely, there is also the search for pure DNA, i.e. the homage. You story respects the genre, its codes, and it allows itself to use references to other works of the genre with finesse. The first risk is plagiarism, and it's a risk that can be economically painful. The second risk, already mentioned, is that of lining up clichés *ad nauseam*. Ultimately, you may end up producing something intended for a niche audience. In the end, you may a beautiful baby, but it's up to you to see the goal you wish to achieve.

HOW TO GAUGE THE CODES?

Avoid a sense of déjà-vu!

We're talking about clichés, typically.

True, we can't reinvent everything, but if you include an interrogation scene with inspectors, you'll need to use another camera angle that's not so stereotypical. You're using the genre's code, which the player is going to identify as such. If she has the sense she's see it a hundred times before and can even anticipate it, it's over. Anticipating a scene is a good cliché detector – so too is annoyance. By nature, a player likes playing, and anticipating and guessing is part of the fun of playing, but it has to be a challenge, a test, a battle, not a "Ah, there you have it, you have do it like this, that's all... "

Pay attention to the equilibrium

We're coming back to the notion of coherence.

If a cliché is "too coherent" in a way, you get bogged down in the genre; if you play with a code and it doesn't hold up, you've blown it. Indeed, codes haven't gradually created a genre for no reason. It's certainly a typology that allows one to orient himself, and if it becomes any old thing, by definition it no longer makes any sense, except if your project is precisely nonsense, but that's something totally different.

How do you play with a code? Often by replacing it with another: if you have fun with the DNA, why not make use of it. You can very well transform interrogation scenes from a crime story into an erotic scene or scene communicating with the beyond. So, you start with a stereotypical scene and you mix it with another. And you can do this if it holds up, if it's coherent. If you're investigator is a nymphomaniac, it's coherent, or if your investigator is a parapsychologist, it's coherent, etc. It's worth pointing out that in the notion of coherence, if the characters bring the story to life, and in particular the character the player is playing, are coherent with their universe, the universe progresses smoothly.

Plan your loop-the-loops

When you do a loop-the-loop in the air, you better know how you're going come out of it, or it's a catastrophe.

And, here, you're working on an interactive story So, when you plan to do a big loop-the-loop with the genre's code, you need to offer the player a sensations, vertigo, especially for switches and other twists.

If you suddenly shift from one genre to another for no reason, it'll turn out badly. In this case, go back over the chapter on revelations. Indeed, if you want to go from crime fiction to zombies, and suddenly, when entering an apartment, the player comes across a bunch of zombies, it's very risky. If it's the beginning of the game, and it's definitely not crime fiction but zombies, and it's going to end up being a survival game or an FPS[6], but right away you sweep aside the crime fiction codes, it could be a disappointment. Whereas if your player has already begun an investigation and the clues (another code of crime fiction) give the impression that something strange is going on, shifting to a zombie universe will be a more or less anticipated surprise, but don't forget that, in this case, the player will be happy to have foreseen the change because it will comfort here abilities to understand your universe. If the player has reason to really sense "some zombies," it's up to you (through your characters, etc.) to give her the taste, or rather the scent.

....

6. *First Person Shooter*, a shooting game from a first-person point of view.

How do I check these three points?

By proofreading. What's all the more complicated with an interactive narrative is that you have to proofread all the different paths.

This proofreading is often a difficult aspect to get others to understand as part of a work order. Creating takes time, but it's not just time spent writing. You have to proofread. This is generally understood. What's harder to get people to understand is that you have to let time pass.

When you write your story, you are inside it, and maybe one day, you're tired and you file into a cliché, maybe playing with this code will bring everything down, maybe your switch is too brutal, but very often, you need to step back to see what sticks out like a sore thumb. And we're telling you, it has to do with your story itself.

Time is essential. To check whether these points are coherent with your universe and, thus, whether you're in control of your codes, you should have someone else have a look. If you have to proofread your work, it's always highly recommended you have someone else proofread it to. If you have little proofreading time, and if you're unable to let time pass to go back over your work later, a proofreader can dive in right away and give you feedback. Be that as it may, the person or persons doing it have to be capable of giving good feedback: a simple "Great!" or "This is garbage!" is not enough.

At the very minimum, follow this rule if you are able to get at least two opinions about your work: similar opinions should get your attention; if your proofreaders say the same thing about a point, if it's positive, you did it right, but if it's negative, maybe you should rework that point. However, differing points of view are hard to use. Maybe it'll make sense to you, and you'll tell yourself he or she is right, and okey-dokey, back to work; maybe you won't agree but it will give you another idea that everyone can agree on, etc.

In any case, you're in the driver's seat. You're the one who decides on what and what not to change. But to check the coherence of a universe, proofreading is indispensable.

The genres: science fiction, crime fiction, horror, etc.

Choice of genre: crime fiction

Relationship with other genres, YES

Story contains more than 50% tof crime fiction codes, okay

Story contains less than 50% of crime fiction codes, hybridization

Cut and paste stories = Plagiarism!

Clichéd story = Boring!

Well placed references: Homage!

Mastery of codes while also play with them: Good story!

Innovative and relevant: Jackpot!

Crossover:
Ex.: Bladerunner,
Banlieue 13,
Robocop,
Time Out, etc.

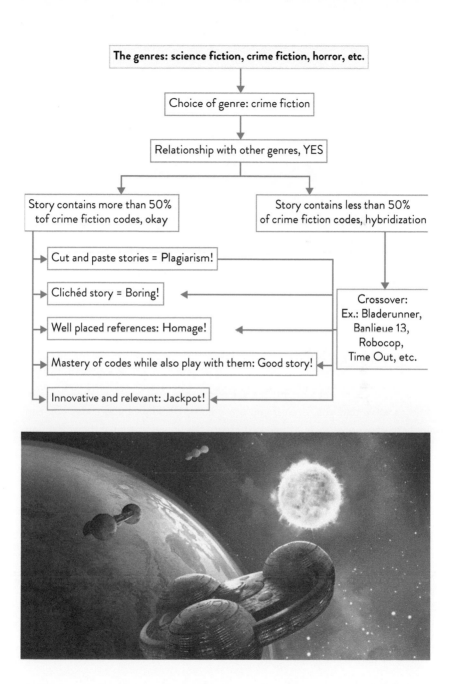

Out There, *the universe of FibreTigre, is a work anchored in European science fiction.*

HOW DO I BUILD A UNIVERSE?

Actually, if you're not working in a specific genre, you ought to think deeper. And as we've told you, even if you use genres, these give you codes you can apply to your universe, but they don't create the universe, even if they offer you some road maps.

PRO INSIGHT

*FibreTigre, how did you manage to maintain coherence in the*Out There *universe throughout the different expansions?*

FibreTigre: It was rather simple, because I work in a very orderly fashion already, I created a ton of signature elements upstream. In *Out There,* it's: scientific realism, European science fiction, no combat, life makes no sense, and a certain dirty, gritty side. By writing with these principles, without even drawing on the key elements of the *Out There* universe, you're able to write something consistent with the universe. After that, you adapt it to the media. a comic book would have different content than a management game.

What universe strategies can you talk to us about?

For a genre like war (we're speaking of war films as much as we are about war games), a game about World War II gives you a universe right way. From there, you go into detail – the whole war or just one year, one country, Europe, Asia?

In crime fiction, you can have the entire story take place at the police head-quarters and use it as a base camp, a focal point and a nexus for the story's intrigues. In the universe of this police headquarters, you'll have polices officers in uniform, inspectors, administrative staff, victims, suspects, etc., but in theory no guilty people – remember that's for the courts to decided.

In your universe mixing crime fiction and zombies, well you'll have the infected area (the cemetery, the hospital, etc.), likewise, the police officers and the zombies won't have the same clothes and equipment, whether it takes place in pres-ent-day France or a British colony in the early 20[th]century.

There's no point in giving more examples, you're universe:

- Serves a scenery for your story
- Provides the back history for your characters

To create it, as soon as you determine where and what period, you need to gather documentation. We're coming back to this stage of the creative process because you don't just create something from nothing, much less a universe.

And imagination? This is your general contractor working for your client, your story. But your imagination is nourished by everything. Even if you want to do something hyper realistic, which sticks to Reality to the millimeter (note the R), it's your imagination that's going to make it happen.

From realism to phantasmagoria...

The need to gather documentation will really depend on your universe. If you want to allow your player to play as a young man in the Middle Ages who's going to become a Franciscan monk and later evangelize in the New World with Las Casas, becoming his confidant, and you want to be as real as possible, you'll need a lot of documentation.

On the other hand, if you just need a monastic environment, regardless of the rites or era, you'll still need documentation, but what will count more is the style and aesthetic of your story, more so than your preoccupation with realism.

In the end, you can write about the life of Flomb de Huihimbo, in the "thirty-twenty-red" century, during the great olfactory Decade. Here, yes, you can grab whatever you want for documentation, you're the sole judge of the reality of this world.

... Just one small thing: coherence

No matter what world or universe you create, coherence is the key word. In general, we accept, even expect extraordinary abilities and acts from a hero or heroine. But they have to be coherent with the universe. Thus, there are two types of coherence: the intrinsic coherence of the universe – in brief, it has to operate on its own – and the character's coherence with it.

Your universe, whether it consists of miserable beggars in the ghettos of 19thcentury London or the feasts and pleasures on the planet Joy, it must coherent, logical. In the first case, your player will easily understand that life is hard, disease is omnipresent, and sordidness and criminal behavior reign. In the other case, it would seem normal to find strange feasts everywhere, people having a good time, endless dancing, orgies, etc.

What isn't logical at is, or expected, must be coherent, explained.

If you put a uranium service station in your London ghetto as a hideout for your miserable characters, this is going to be a central part of your story, here, because you're going to have to explain this to the player. This isn't a normal thing at all in the universe you've chosen.

Likewise, on planet Joy, a jukebox that only plays songs by Wehrmacht is not innocuous.

So, you can create a universe, but anything that seems atypical needs to be related to your story. Otherwise, you're going to create frustration and may even forfeit the credibility of your universe: in summary, that's nonsense.

Do well to understand that the universe serves your stories, and not the other way around, at least in most cases. You can make a long novel, a video game saga, anything where the evolution of the universe takes priority over everything else. Read *Helliconia* by Bran Aldiss, the hero (we'll come back to the notion of the main character) is the planet, it's unchanging cycle. In a strict sense it's a *planet opera*. Even when the universe is the central subject, more than ever, you need to avoid incoherence.

True, you can have some elements of mystery, which might become cult. But beware of anything that turn out to be an error in consistency, an anachronism, etc.

If you want a hyper-real universe, naturally you will avoid incoherences that undermine your universe's credibility. Take care not to make a documentary, however. One of the biggest difficulties, when gathering documentation, is to chose the moment to stop gather information so you can start your story. And here, you're the one who decides: if knowing the number of steps it takes to reach the San Sebastian cathedral is irrelevant to your story, then forget about it.

Your universe, whether real or phantasmagoric, must serve your story.

PRO INSIGHT

Sybil, how do you manage the coherence of a creative universe?

Sybil Collas: If you're talking about a creative universe as a *"lore"* (the universe, the rules and the myths a game is based on), there are three elements: documentation, coherence and human intelligence. Building a bible for the universe is imperative for any creator of worlds, and it requires a lot of involvement.

When you work as a writer on a development team, it's important to consider that the documentation isn't a resource for you, but rather for others: you have to treat all information as if it were intended for the other developers and make sure it's in line with their specific constraints. To ensure coherence in the game, coherence in the documentation is not enough: you need document that answers the questions of the people who are going to read it, not your own questions. Abandon long paragraphs describing the back story and highlight the relevant tools and informations for the animators (rare emotions and frequent emotions, body language), for voice actors (age, accent, mannerisms, obsessions) for the artists responsible for the environment (elements of the story in the scenery, how the environment is used in the story, symbolic meanings, connections with the characters and the other environments), for the dialogue writers, the game designers, the sound designers, etc. – and this list is far from exhaustive. You are not the only guardian of game coherence and you, thus, must give the whole team the ability to create and maintain this coherence, no matter if the team consists of two people or a hundred.

Naturally, it's about production capacity. When you are under time or budget constraints, it's up to you to identify the points for which coherence is not indispensable and the points you want to concentrate on. You really have to train yourself to recognize these fundamental elements because they form the foundation of the topics and the universe of your story.

Joe, how do you manage the coherence of a creative universe when adapting an IP (intellectual property) to an interactive story?

Joe Pinney: I read and watch everything I can about the IP and try to get to know the universe inside and out. If possible, I stay in contact with the IP creators and get their input. I also listen to the reactions of its biggest fans around me.

Trust you player, your audience

Normally, your player has little idea of what she's going to experience, or what's at stake, it's a total surprise. As you know, she expects to be a heroine, so, yes, she expects to experience some extreme situations, both horrible and magnificent. And if that's connected to the universe, it's perfect.

And your player has a precise expectation. If we ask offer the experience to relive as accurately as possible the adventure of an Inuit whaler 200 years ago, then, yes, she's going to want and expect a detailed, meticulous universe.

On the other hand, if she has to face a horde of goblins attacking a castle, first off, she will be less demanding on the universe's details as they compare to reality. It's up to you to refine the genealogy of each goblin warrior and the initiation rituals of each tribe. Always ask yourself the question: how does this information serve my story? Do I really have a need for it? Can knowing that the youngest goblins aren't allowed to use swords, for example, help me survive in the castle? If not, it's just goblin ethnology. That said, it's not like it has to go straight to the trash.

You can expect a player playing as an Inuit whaler, moved by her own curiosity, to ask the shaman questions and expect him, when asked, to sing a divination chant.

In other cases, the player's first priority is to finish the game, to win, etc.

After that, everything you've created to fill out the universe, think about how you're going to reveal it. This is fundamental if these revelations serve the story. This is secondary if they enhance the universe. In the case of our goblins, the young goblins' problem can be conveyed by a warrior – let's be efficient – but it's not fundamental. You can allow the player to walk down the castle hall and stop to read the chronicles of the head goblins whose portraits are hanging on a wall.

We are getting ahead of ourselves with the part about the revelations, but once a universe is created, because it can be a colossal task, you need to choose where to direct your efforts, and thus prioritize and develop what will be presented directly to the player.

The player more or less details on the environment depending on her need for them, or not, to succeed at the game. If your game consists of shooting at targets, the universe is just a scenery for you to hang your targets on. Now, if your game consists of find a target, the right target, the depth of the universe can add credibility to your story.

A credible universe for a credible story

If, in your world, everyone dies as soon as they touch a drop of water, if some characters act hale and hearty in the shower and there's no logical explanation with respect to the universe, then it's all wrong. If the heroine of this world has the power to take showers and her enemies search for others with the same mutation, this becomes logical, coherent.

One thing that is typically admitted in video games, games, and interactive storytelling is the heroine's will power and resistance.

Even in a contemporary universe, your police officer, your soldier, the player expects to be able to take blows or fight without ever sleeping or taking a breather. And it's the same for the big villains. It's normal to make them extraordinary beings. There's plenty to be said about the notion of the superman in games. But you need to remember this especially, it seems coherent for the player to do extraordinary things in the universe because she is the heroine. But your universe will nevertheless define the limits. For example, your character, despite having 100,000 hit points, jumps off a cliff and dies. If your character doesn't die, you'll need an explanation right away, otherwise this is incoherent.

And the accumulation of incoherences makes your universe less credible, just like an incoherent universe makes a story less credible.

FibreTigre, what sense do you give to your different creations?

FibreTigre: There is always a basic theme. *Out There* said "Life is an accident, all is in vain." *Out There II*, the sequel, said: "Finally, all is perhaps not in vain, nothing is." *Antioch* describes a social, psychological, French approach to the police investigation. *Firebird* poses the question of whether the past is a shelter...

It's a great question that's never explicit in the story but it's one that is answered in the telling.

World expansion and end

In your coherent universe, not everything has to be explained if it has a logical place. We can easily imagine a catholic mission abandoned in your New World and your evangelical monk passes by but, because he's in a hurry, he doesn't stop. But maybe you can use this later for another story or development. You write interactive stories, perhaps you haven't had the time to use everything you wanted to. You've respected the project specifications but maybe you have some extra ideas? No problem, maybe one day this abandoned mission will serve you as a point of entry where you can add a branch.

Whether an entire world or a sordid family environment, you've created a universe, right? Now destroy it! You're there to offer an experience, an interactive adventure. Saving the world is good, destroying it can also offer a good story. In particular, think about it when you read the part about trigger events, or revelations. What you've taken care to create (a cyclone, for example) may also give you numerous potential interactions among your characters.

Speaking of cyclones, you're writing interactive narrative. This means you can offer several universes, develop alternative forms of your universe, but be careful you don't get swept away by the task: everything must serve your story and, quite often, your main character(s).

Ah, let's talk about this, precisely.

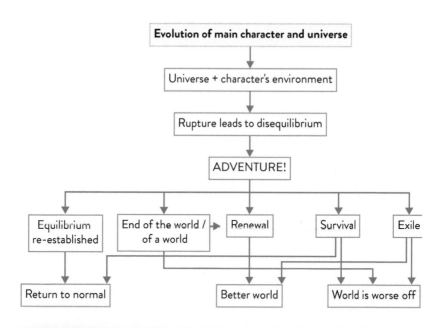

A coherent universe is a credible universe	
Example, universal rule: the sun kills vampires	
1 Vampires don't go out at night.	coherent
2 Vampires meet at the beach at noon.	incoherent
3 Vampires meet at the beach at noon because they have a special protection.	coherent
Stretching the limits of a universe	
Example, universal rule: superheroes exist.	
1 A superhero falls from a building and gets back up.	coherent, he's a superhero.
2 A superhero falls from a planet and dies.	coherent, the player understands that he reached the limits of his universe.
3 The superhero falls from a planet and uses something new and survives. The consequences change everything.	coherent, the player understands that the superhero just stretched the limits of his universe.

The rich, coherent universe of Might & Magic,
that Erwan Le Breton work on as the creative director.

8. THE MAIN CHARACTER

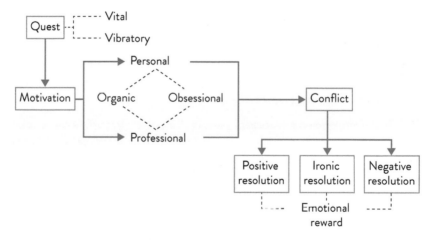

The main character, to be brief, is driven by a quest that must resonate throughout his entire body. The call to adventure is too strong. The stakes driving him must be vital. Next, you need to continually motivate this character in order to involve your player. *Why is it so essential to go all out?* Motivating the character means having him face a series of Cornelian dilemmas[7]. This is how twists

....

7. In 1637 *Le Cid* was written by the man who gave his name to a typical dilemma. Corneille's play tells the story of Rodrigo, torn between love and country (in this particular case vengeance).

and turns appear, the purpose of which is to cause the character trouble. The stronger the conflict, the more gripping the quest. The final resolution depends on your player's numerous choices. The more you successfully keep the story's promises, the greater the emotional reward will be.

A good interactive story is a story where the player has the sensation that the story was written just for her.

We could also call the main character a hero or heroine, but there are also anti-heroes. In sum, in any case, it's your main character. He or she is who your player will play as.

This is the most interesting, most complex character, the one that is going to carry the action. Don't fret about trying to making him human: make him exciting, fascinating! A character has two important characteristics: he is an orphan, in the sense that he feels alone, in a strict and figurative sense, and he has convictions, in the sense that he fights to achieve his dreams (whether a voyage or vengeance).

Note that a profoundly good character whose quest is legitimate, just and good is often profoundly annoying. *Sometimes*, because Zelda, you have to admit, was capable of making our childhood delightful. Even so, players are also drawn to the darkness lying dormant within each of us. Characters are lies, cowards and outcasts, too. Offer the play the chance to explore this spectrum.

Red Dead Redemption is a successful game in all aspects. First off, because John Marston is a charismatic, somber and intelligent character. While the choices (almost) don't have any consequence, the player dreads each action and measures each movement carefully. Of course, there isn't just John Marston, there are other complex secondary characters, thrilling quests and open world chock full of surprises. That's all!

Whoever dared fire on his own horse, give yourself up!

This is a very powerful game that goes straight into the top 5 westerns of all time, next to Sergio Leone, Sam Peckinpah and Raoul Walsh.

ONE OR TWO MAIN CHARACTERS?

The question is worthing asking. In most cases, your player plays a character, but it's not uncommon either, and interactive storytelling can lend itself, with the many choices to be made, for the player to play as different main characters in a consecutive fashion. This is the case, for example, with the excellent *Tales from Borderlands*. In literature, this is generally referred to as a choral novel, you will have different main characters, who sometimes live parallel lives, in which some elements will only serve as bridge between them.

Whether you have one or several main characters, creating each one is going to follow the same rules and have the same needs. Remember that a character is a vehicle by which your player will journey through your story and choose different branches. The player is in command. That's one of the particular features of an interactive story, and it mustn't be forgotten when creating your main character – she can even "break" your main character.

You can very well create a character whose adventure will be interesting to read or watch, but not to play – this would be the case, for example, of a character so strongly marked by destiny that his choices, when all is said and done, lead only to his perdition. Remember that you are making a game, a game with multiple endings, and even if all the endings lead to the perdition of the main character(s), one has to have the desire to play them.

You undoubtedly know how to create a universe, you have perhaps read the corresponding chapter; your character is at all times connected to this universe. You will understand that, for now, for simplicity's sake, we will speak only of one main character.

PRO INSIGHT

David, do you prefer to write a story for a unique character like in Beyond : Two Souls, *or stories with several characters, like* Heavy Rain *or* Detroit*?*

David Cage: Honestly, I like both. They are two very different things. I like working on several characters because it gives you the opportunity to have different points of view in one story. It also allows you to quickly change situations and scenes before the player has the time to get bored.

More generally, it's not about what I prefer to do or not to do. It's really the story, the topic and the characters you create that will tell you what the narrative needs. I prefer when the story tells me what it needs rather than dictating the story. I think that each author must know how to listen to their story.

Joe, can you talk to us about your characters' motivations and conflicts?

Joe Pinney: I particularly work with other people's characters, with licensed intellectual property and with writing partners. I look for personal relationships to help me feel my character's motivations. When I write my own characters, I take inspiration from people I know well and from myself. This is the best way I know for things to remain true.

Thomas, talk to us about your main characters' motivations and conflicts? How did you create them?

Thomas Veauclin: All the characters of *The Council* are main characters. They all have a raison d'être, commitments and hidden desires. We worked on two different planes, the internal motivations and the exterior motivations. They also have strengths and weaknesses. Most of them are connected to one or more characters in the game, and it's up to the player to reveal the web.

What role do the secondary characters play?

We don't have secondary characters. We have twelve main characters. Period. We've attempted to recreate a close meeting where all the guests have their place. And from a production standpoint, our slogan was: make small but make quality. So, few characters, but well made.

BRINGING IT TO LIFE

Your main character is your baby, and when you see what scriptwriters usually put their heroes through, well, you may have doubts about their parenting abilities. In any case, this is the character you're going to be the most attentive to.

Generally, you already have a pretty solid idea about the characters, particularly your main character, in your eventual story. Obviously, if this is for a work order, and if your hero or heroine already exists, this will go faster. You'll either have authorization to modify the character, or you'll have to respect the status quo.

Your main character must be coherent on two points: its universe and itself. It is not uncommon for the universe to revolve around the main character, but it is not a firm rule. What's import for you to remember is that your main character must have a good reason to be there. Later, if this universe has already been presented to players in other stories, you'll quickly have to ask yourself whether your character is consistent or not with the chronology of this universe, the past episodes and the character's place in this universe. If we take the Marvel universe, we can create a new superhero, but we'll have to situate him well among the impressive array of other superheroes already present, and what this world has experienced.

Your character may be disruptive. He's been catapulted into a universe and, naturally, he's going to save it or destroy it. This is the type of main character who normally shouldn't be there, and it's a strong springboard for your story. The character's motivation will sometimes be to get back home. Ah, that, the motivation, we'll have a chance to come back to that in more detail later.

If it's coherent with your universe, the main character must also be coherent. This is obvious, but if you create a soldier, everyone will be surprised if she lacks bravery. From here, you have to explain it to the players because everything that'll characterize your main character is going to be an element of the game. So, be attentive to coherence if your soldier is the most cowardly of the whole regiment – the player needs to know why because there will be numerous choices related to this attribute. Do not neglect skills: if your solder is a specialist in placing securities on the stock exchange, there has to be a good reason for this type of surprise. Aside from this, feel free to create a companion for her who's an arms dealer that showed her the secrets of the trade.

Once you have these two points about coherence in mind, move on to characterization.

CHARACTERIZING YOUR MAIN CHARACTER: MOTIVATE IT!

Whether your heroine is a super soldier or a Neptunian bulldog, you have to thoroughly define your main character. It's not just about character traits, but also skills, physique, attitude, behavior, etc.

And consequently, unless you're making a three-day old baby, you address the main character's past, and this is what will have the most positive or negative repercussions in your universe. And if your heroine is a three-day old baby, the past is even more important. Three-day old Superman is not just any baby. He'll just avoid little jars of kryptonite, that's all.

The essential point to developing your main character, even if it's a toaster, is its motivation: why is it going to experience this adventure and commit to it?

The motivation may be intrinsic, it's part of its nature, it had it at from the start of the adventure. Perhaps it wants to make the best toasted bread possible? Perhaps our super soldier wants to become a general, avenge the colonies on

Beta Epsilon in Quadrant Six, or find a chest full of gold forgotten by the Nazis (it's crazy what stuff these guys have left behind according to scriptwriters)? The motivation is inside the character. Aside from that, this may just be what leads to the adventure, and when you character has to flee a band of aliens or Nazis, the motivation will be survival.

The advantage of survival as a motivation is the you can easily lead a character there. But careful, we insist on coherence. If you're making a comedy adventure, one will easily understand if a vacuum salesman turns out to be a true survivor, while this will be less coherent in a realistic universe, i.e. a survivalist's universe.

Your character's motivation must not disturb the coherence of the universe. It must become your player's motivation. Is this really the case? In a shoot 'em up, it's like your player's motivation will be the score, or some particularly vicious shots, etc. and the character's motivation, for example vengeance, will take a back seat.

It all depends on what effect you want to give to the story, but careful: telling yourself "no need to go overboard offering a good, motivated main character that'll ultimately serve as nothing more than an avatar while the player does whatever she wants" is the best way to create an boring character and a game that is just as boring. The player can do whatever the hell she wants, you can even penalize her for it, but you, you can't do whatever the hell you want. You, you're making a good interactive story. Otherwise, the penalty for you will be worse than just *game over*.

So, you need to motivate your heroine, in line with the universe and the tone of the story you're going to develop, and if the motivation chances due to such or such branch, you must motivate, if we may dare say, this new motivation.

So, maybe you develop your main character a ton and then you only keep the elements that serve the story and the game. This doesn't mean you throw the rest, all the "fat," in the garbage and only keep a few choice cuts. This isn't the case.

First, what you've developed has certainly helped you create or fill out your universe. Indeed, one of the best aways of ensuring coherence between the two – the main character and the universe of the story – is to let them evolve together.

The additional elements you have that don't influence the main storyline, or rather storylines, can be elements that the play will learn about from a conversation with another character, or by discovering a document, etc. Any player who wants to learn more about the heroine's and the universe's past – and this isn't uncommon when someone plays an interactive story – may like taking time to discover the side stories. All this is to be considered, unless, however, it isn't this type of project, i.e. your story doesn't direct the player toward the past but rather toward resolving the plot. To avoid this, for example, you can refer to the part of this book about trigger events.

We've said it before, the substantive things you create for your heroine serve as so many anchor points to build ties among the secondary characters, whether those ties are already present, form at the start of the adventure, or develop over the course of the story. What can be woven can be unraveled. An interest in interactive storywriting is playing on the relationships among the characters: if your heroine does not motivate her team, she may see it break up, for example.

PRO INSIGHT

David, how do you create characters and their motivations?

David Cage: More than anything else, a good story hinges on its charac-ters. To my mind, one of the most important things is to arouse empathy between the player and your characters. If you don't give a damn about your characters, you don't give a damn about what happens to them and won't feel any emotion: the narrative experience falls flat. So, I always try to establish this empathy with the player. I don't think there's a magic recipe.

Personally, I try to write characters that are as human as possible. Even when I'm working on an android, I try to give him something that will make the player say: "Oh yeah, okay, it resembles me a little in that way" or "I understand why it's acting like that."

You've spoken about empathy, how do you arouse empathy in the player?

You absolutely want your player to put himself in the main character's shoes. That's why I avoid giving superpowers to my characters or make them to powerful because I think that it creates a distance between the character and the player.

It's very important to give enough exposure time to the characters. You need time to meet them and care about them before something dramatic can happen to them. Sometimes, I see stories, often in games, where a character goes through something dramatic right in the very first sequence. How can I care about that character when I don't even know anything about it? That simply doesn't work at all.

Taking time to expose your characters is always somewhat complicated in a game because a lot of players like stories to start off strong. They want explosions, adrenaline, a "wow effect" in the first seconds. Personally, most often I find that it's better to start calmly, smoothly.

In *Heavy Rain*, for example, the game starts during the hero's daily routine: he wakes up, brushes his teeth, starts working on his architecture plans... when something powerful happens to the character, the player is moved because he knows the character and is able to identify with him in some way or another.

FibreTigre, talk to us about your main characters' motivations and conflicts. How did you create them?

FibreTigre: I have some characters motivated by violent passions or rigid principles that nevertheless know how to remain human. It's enough to leave them with their passions and their personalities, and they write themselves. Many people just want to be reassured, to be loved, to care for their psychological wounds, and I like writing stories where the characters treat themselves with the adventure.

HOW TO HAVE AN IDEA
OF THE RIGHT FORMULA

Your main character, as we've already mentioned, can be the universe of your story, such as a *planet opera*. This can be an ocean, a forest, etc. Even in these cases, characterization will mean defining the ecosystem – what does your ocean fear (pollution, etc.), what is threatening your forest (termites, etc.)?

On the other hand, this could be a police officer, the manager of the fresh foods section of a large supermarket, with their strengths, their weaknesses, their aspirations, etc.

So, how do I know if I have a good main character once I've done the molding, the mock up, the psychological profile, the press kit, etc.? There is a good way, which we describe for you below.

The challenge

You main character has to be suitable for accepting the challenge you're proposing in your interactive story. Remember that it's the player who's in control, not you anymore.

So, if your police officer is invulnerable, super smart, in sum, if the adventure proposed is a cakewalk, or worse, if we wonder why he was even interested in such a pathetic investigation in the first place, well, your character is a bust. Careful, don't get us wrong, anyhow, you get it. You can create your super handsome invulnerable hunk with the idea of taking the opposite approach and, precisely, make him fall. Here, your character is suitable because he's not expecting the challenge he's going to have to take on.

Always remember that your player is going to be playing. A too powerful character is just as bad as a character who has an asthma attack as soon as he climbs a set of stairs in a universe where there's stairs everywhere.

It's a game: you can obviously play with the difficulties of the tests, etc. But if your character is very powerful, consequently you end up trying to outdo yourself with tests in order to give him something in proportion with his dimensions, so be attentive to coherence with the universe... On the other hand, if you make up for your character's defects by giving him reserves of Albuterol at each stage, what was the purpose of making him so fragile and weak?

Your character must fit the adventure he's going to experience, and the ups and downs that come with it. Plus, you're writing an interactive script, so you have the chance to make certain routes increasingly more difficult or increasingly more easy, depending on the player's choices.

However, we cannot repeat it enough, you have to remain consistent. So, yes, if your player is playing Athena, goddess of Mt. Olympus, one can expect her to challenge the Titans all day long, but, and other chapters address this subject, there is nothing worse than boring the player. That's the risk oneupmanship.

You can offer some predictable passages for your character, to pay lip service to fans, you can offer surprises, challenges, but you must always make sure the character being played has a good reason to be there.

You're a hero, or an anti-hero, or you're not.

And the character traits?

You need motivation to write your story, and you need to know what will motivate your main character. Eventually, this depends on your game, the player, herself, can choose from different motivations at the start. After all, you're writing the interactivity. However, in addition there are inevitably different stories to be made, and don't forget that you have to produce a narrative. So, think carefully before choosing this kind of option.

On the other hand, it is easier to adjust the character's personality, to let the player to develop for herself, based on her taste, the relationships among the characters and, thus, play on the character traits, the personality. That being said, you can propose subtle nuances if, for the sake of your story, you have a need to retain such or such trait, but don't for any reason deprive the player of the ability to respond with several choices and several attitudes. This seems obvious, but play with the player. You can offer her, on a regular basis, punchlines that she is free to use or not.

This will have a lesser interest if the interactions with the others involve confrontation. But even in this case, in the options for the player's attitude, you can make her play based on the character's traits: she spares the wounded, she punches weakly, etc.

Bear in mind that character traits are only conveyed in dialogues.

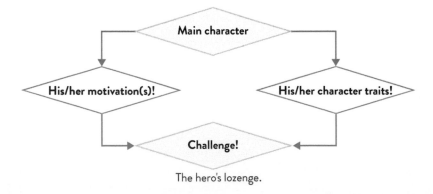

The hero's lozenge.

Jean-Luc, how do you build your main character?

Jean-Luc Cano: I always build it as it relates to the topic, and I never build it alone but rather as it relates to the other characters. In general, I build my hero and his corresponding adversary because they are the same. They have the same goal, but not the same way of achieving it, unless one of them is right and the other is wrong. The adversary must have an intelligent discourse because the audience must only feel one thing: empathy. When there is a true bad guy, but people comprehend him, it's a success.

Do you have any archetypal characters?

We always meet archetypal characters. As opposed to caricatures, which is a lack of work, easy, the archetype serves to anchor a character in the collective comprehension: a prince who wants to become king, for example. This type of archetype can be transformed in endless ways: with a soccer team, an intern at a company, etc. The heart of the story is the character. The spectator identifies not with a universe, or a city, but with a character.

Connor, Kara and Markus are the main characters of Detroit: Become Human
(Quantic Dream).

9. CREATE A NETWORK OF SECONDARY CHARACTERS

Unless you're making a radical choice, your secondary characters will help define what your character is like.

THE EXTRAS

It's better if we talk about this right away to address this topic. This is about characters, like in a film, who are there more so for the universe than for the role they play. The bystanders, the guards, in sum all the characters whose interaction is minimal, in the sense that the player will not establish any relationship with them through the main character.

Your player can spend a long time eliminating a guard, but, in and of itself, you don't have to define this character if its only role in the story is to represent a minor test. Confronting the interplanetary drug kingpin's right-hand man is another thing. You are certainly up against a secondary character.

THE WORLD OF SUPPORTING ROLES

You have all the supporting roles of the main character's entourage (if any). But here again, they must serve the story. If we perhaps have a need to know the first name's of the heroine's parents, or their profession, to fill out the character's past, it's not necessary to do so for the extras.

Don't turn members of the main character's entourage into supporting actors. They're going to have an influence on the story or may already have one. You're doing interactive script writing. There is a strong likelihood that your player's choices will exclude certain characters, relegating them.

How do I characterize them?

Since you'll most in cases you'll have more secondary characters than main characters, it's pointless to characterize them in detail. You can if you want, but time is a precious commodity. And if you fill out a secondary character, you'll have more and more difficulty leaving it in the background.

This is one of the difficulties: your player's main character takes priority. If a secondary character is going to have an important role, it must not however eclipse the main character. Here is a good way to see whether you have the right formula: if secondary character is always getting the heroine out of a bind, this may throw your story out of balance.

So develop them just as much as necessary. If there are files for these characters in the game (police files, personnel files, etc.), in this case it's an element of the game, and you need to develop them. It's hard to imagine an investigation game where the suspects are defined in two words or less.

So, think carefully about the genre you're using, whether you're using one or two genres in your story. Not the least because the advantage of genres is to offer you archetypes.

Archetype

We only use them in stories of such and such a genre, but it's a good place to find some.

In a western, you will often have the quick-shooting hit man, or the alcoholic sheriff, etc. In a slasher film, there will be young women who prefer to scream instead of fleeing the serial killer.

Archetypes allow you to quickly define your secondary character (daring pilot, Vietnam vet, mad scientist, etc.)

Obviously, the risk is that your character will be a cliché, i.e. the umpteenth femme fatale à la film noir, the umpteenth alien laying eggs in a human body, etc.

There is where you need your archetype to be coherent with your universe but also bring something extra to it. Your femme fatale is an old detective turned transsexual, your alien only lays eggs in humans who's body temperature is only 100.4°F, etc.

In addition to the traits that are going to give your archetype a little shine, there is obviously the connection with the main character.

You're writing an interactive narrative, so the player can do what she wants, in theory. But if you make a fuss about creating your secondary characters to make them stand out from the extras, they need to be important elements to the plot. If the player does not see the femme fatale, she won't have any information to make her life easier. If the player doesn't run into the egg-laying alien, she won't understand why all the victims have the same temperature, etc.

Your secondary characters are there to be allies or enemies and may, depending on the player's choices in particular, change sides along the way – in certain universes the line between good and evil is often blurred, a little like in ours...

PRO INSIGHT

David, do you have any archetypes in mind?

David Cage: I love working with archetypes, even though the line between archetypes and clichés can prove to be very fine. People sometimes confuse the two, but I think that, more than anything, a cliché is a character you've seen a thousand times that doesn't surprise you. You get to the end of the story, and the character is exactly what you expected.

An archetype, on the other hand, is a character who seems familiar but is just a point of entry that will ultimately take you somewhere you weren't expecting to go.

In *Detroit*, the most popular character is by far Connor for more than 50% of the players. Connor is a typical archetype you have already seen dozens of times in games, films or books. He's a rookie cop who has to work with a veteran cop, and they can't stand each other. This story has been told countless times, and if it stopped there, the players wouldn't have appreciated would have been nothing more than a cliché. It turned the players loved this duo because the story makes them take unexpected twists sprinkled with humor while you learn more about them and their relationship.

Witnesses

Your secondary characters also serve to highlight your main character. They witness his heroism, or infamy, depending on the story or the player's choices. Indeed, they make it possible to show the player that her choices have consequences, whether predictable or not, whether irreversible or not.

It's thanks to these secondary characters – if we take, for example, a main character other than a survivor in a desolated place – that the player knows what moral direction they are taking their character in. A moral direction that can be suitable (or not if desired) for your universe. In a universe of mercenaries, in terms of coherence and the player's expectations, your secondary characters may witness your character's professionalism or amateurism, his human side or, just the opposite, his wild side, but it's very unlikely that you'll lead your character off somewhere to become a midwife or Buddhist monk (even John Rambo didn't manage that). Your secondary characters would certainly be surprised by such a direction. Thus, if your heroine mercilessly executes her prisoners, your secondary characters can react.

You see, they serve the plot by opposing or helping the main character, but there is an entirely human aspect that allows you to make the universe denser and bolster the player's gaming experience. And you're the one who controls, in part, the situation. You can decide that eating babies on a spit is well looked upon by demons of the 7th circle, for example, and they will bear witness to it.

Don't forget that the game, the story, is focused on the player. She's the one who experiences the story, so the secondary characters must be looking at her. And if they aren't from the very beginning, the player's actions are going to lead her to notice this.

In our western, the quick-shooting hit man would eventually hear of our young trigger-happy champion – perhaps he even laughed in her face the first time he saw her and has bitterly regretted it since.

Secondary characters for secondary missions

First off, your secondary characters can have their own objectives. But their own objectives must hinge on the player's, or oppose them. If your femme fatale wants to find the creep who killed the surgeon who helped her with her sex change – and if in your story, this never concerns the player to a greater or lesser degree – it's a bust.

Next, your secondary characters have the right profile, as friends or enemies, to propose secondary missions, which is common in interactive stories. The player may not have all the elements to determine whether it's secondary in regard to her story or not, but she can play this mission and get something out of it, and this something must always have a consequence on her own adventure. This can be as simple as a weapon that will help her eliminate her opponents as fast as possible or a newspaper clipping giving her additional information about the past of the serial killers she's hunting down.

If you create secondary missions connected with your secondary characters and these missions don't have anything to do with the player's story, no matter what the preceding choices have been, you're creating frustration and doubt. At the end of the game, the player is going to think she missed something even though that's not the case. Frustrating the player allows you to motivate her to continue playing, but under no circumstances must this be the final sentiment!

A solid network

Your secondary characters can have connections amongst themselves, whether it's hate, lover or any other type of relationship. The more you move the game in this direction, the more you underscore the social relationships. For example, targeting someone's daughter is rarely a good idea, and if you gave an ass kicking to a young girl at the beginning, running into her four-star general father later on will obviously not go so well. Conversely, the femme fatale will undoubtedly thank you for not teaming up with the guy she suspects of killing her surgeon.

If your secondary characters are the witnesses of the player's main role, making her intervene in their relationships reinforces the player's importance in the universe, and her experience. She can help the four-star general's daughter to stop acting like a spoiled brat. Or show the femme fatale that her surgeon died in an accident and that she should cooperate with the man she suspected. The team building aspect can be interesting to develop, and not just a phase intended to recruit the skills needed to achieve an objective.

Is the big villain a secondary character?

Yes, because he isn't played by the player. No, because he's the big villain. Plus, there can be several of them, and they can have a whole ton of deadly henchmen, each more bizarre than the next. You need to take care of your player's opponents. That's part of the challenge, and the fun.

Even if you're not going for a *manu militari* kill 'em all angle, you need to make sure, however, that your oil magnate or tyrannical ship captain don't make the captain of the *Bounty* look like a pushover.

You mustn't assume that a secondary character means the this is an insipid, weak and uninteresting, a buffoon who makes the hero look better. The secondary characters can dominate your main character's world and universe, but, unluckily for them, the story revolves around the main character, and it's your player who is going to live all that.

Once again, careful with clichés. If you cut and paste another Darth Vader or Machiavellian Lord Lannister, it'll be a bust. There is nothing worse than unappealing interchangeable opponents.

Naturally, so what do you do? It's always about involving the player, playing on the character's motivation. We're not going to topple a tyrant to restore freedom. We've seen that one and a thousand times. Your main character has a good reason to oppose a secondary character on par with the big villains. Which doesn't mean that great ideals are verboten, but they must be in your character's DNA or otherwise you'll have to insert them during the adventure, generally during a defining moment for the player.

Marking a milestone

In their role as witnesses, secondary characters also serve to mark milestones in the adventure. By their arrival in the story, they show that the storyd is evolving, just as when they leave. Indeed, they are not all necessarily destined to accompany the main character all the way to the end.

First, if there are opponents, eliminating them, or hunting them down, sets the pace the game. The player's allies can mark a milestone in the story with their disappearance and can, if possible, have consequences on the player's decisions. A disappearance doesn't necessarily have to be brutal, but the character may decide to no longer collaborate, *bye, bye!*

Based on the player's experience, what happens to secondary characters (a marriage, a death, etc.) can, must have an impact on her. For better or for worse, she can be relieved by a happy outcome or shed a burden.

Moving forward in a story doesn't just happen by going from one place to another. If your story has secondary characters, their evolution, and thus their relationships with the main character, generates different stages and moves the story along.

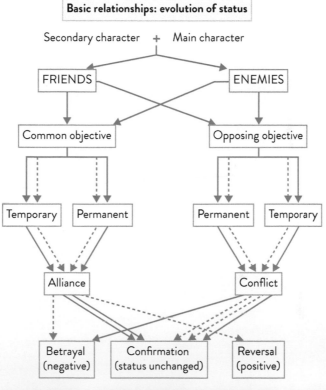

Basic relationships: evolution of status

Secondary character + Main character

FRIENDS — ENEMIES

Common objective — Opposing objective

Temporary | Permanent — Permanent | Temporary

Alliance — Conflict

Betrayal (negative) — Confirmation (status unchanged) — Reversal (positive)

The web of secondary characters in The Council, created by Thomas Veauclin,
is the keystone of this story-driven, historical drama.

10. TRIGGER EVENTS AND REVELATIONS

TRIGGER EVENTS

You're writing an interactive story, and, in order to have something to tell, something better well happen.

The trigger event is what's going to kick-start your story, give it a push. We can talk about just one trigger event, but it's also quite possible to have several of them in one story, particularly in an interactive story.

First of all, depending on your player's choices, you can offer her different trigger events to start the adventure. It is also possible to use them over the course of the game, although in this case, they're intended to resume the plot or announce a radical change in the story. Remember that in interactive script writing, things are less set in stone than normal. You can also do a switch, i.e. make a 180° turn, in sum, offer more twists and turns, since your player needs to feel that her choices influence the universe. Careful though, a trigger event doesn't originate from the consequences of the player's choices – you're the one who planned an event in the story to offer such or such important aspect in the plot.

The purpose of spreading out these trigger events is to move the story forward. There is the interventionist phenomenon, the player can't do anything about it, but you're there to offer her a coherent story, so there better well be some things out of her control that happen, too – simply put, the event must lead the player to take more interest in the game, otherwise it will be a dud.

The first trigger event

This is the trigger event that will start your story. Recovering a couple of droids (a young man and an old man) in your space ship doesn't trigger much, at worst a run-in with authorities. If you're a smuggler, this is a normal thing you do. On the other hand, arriving at your destination in an asteroid field and realizing that your passengers' planet has been blown to pieces, that, that starts and adventure, here you have a trigger event. If you're playing the role of the smuggler.

If you're playing the young man who boards this ship, the trigger event is that you bought the droids from some kind of native scrap merchant, you have a habit of haggling with them, even getting attacked for being a looter isn't by itself out of the normal, even though, clearly, thing's are getting tense. But when your foster family is massacred, we're definitely at a trigger event here.

We'll see further on, the first trigger event is the first point of no return.

Is this necessarily a tragic event?

You can play a single woman who is invited to a wedding – in itself, socially, there is nothing strange, you're a family member or a friend of the family. There, you meet a man you, really, like. Things move in a positive direction. You give him your number, and later he calls you. Do you pick up or not? Here, you have a trigger event.

The first trigger event must lead the player to make a radical choice. The player must realize that the adventure is there, at her door. She may have perceived it earlier (the cheap droids, an aggressive looter, fugitive customers, going to the wedding or not), but the trigger event gives her a choice, the consequences of which are serious. She feels it. Here's why it's connected with a point of no return.

Answering the call of adventure or not

In interactive script writing, as opposed to other stories, you are not required to make the player face a tragic choice, hands and feet bound. She can reject the adventure, it's up to you to see if she can reject it once, twice, etc.

Here's why, in the above examples, the potentially fatal consequences to the choices put her back against the wall. Flee the planet or go into hiding, knowing that the second option doesn't look good. Turn around with the passengers or approach the small moon? But something isn't right at all... Picking up or not your suitor's call is also a way for the heroine to reject or not the call of adventure. And your player will understand the stakes very well.

Always remember that as opposed to the main characters in other types of stories, the main character of an interactive story is (or at least it appears) is more free to make choices, since there is a player in him. And this player often has an idea of the stakes she's playing for. If she chooses and adventure in a galaxy far, far away, she expects some tragic situations, situations involving action, whereas if she is playing a romance, she expects more psychological situations, more hesitations, before she dances the boogie-woogie or not with a Slovenian curling champion.

The trigger event can also be a surprise. If you play a Vietnam veteran going to see an old brother in arms, and if you wander the streets like a vagabond and aren't surprised when you get stopped by the police, you certainly don't imagine at all that you could be thrown in the slammer out of precaution and be treated like cattle.

Event or incident?

One can debate about this for a long time, but us, we prefer trigger event to trigger incident. Simply because in interactive script writing, you have to mark the moment when the player has to realize she's facing something that is going to take her character out of the ordinary, a very variable ordinary, depending on whether an aesthetician or a troll warrior is playing.

A trigger incident is more like a little conflict leads to another until it snowballs into something big. There's that sheriff who takes you to the other side of the village and drops you off on the outskirts, that looter surprises you and almost robs your landspeeder, or that wedding announcement in your mailbox. The more incidents you put before the event, the more you've decided to work on the atmosphere, setting up your universe and your characters.

But don't forget that an event has to occur because if the setup takes an eternity, the player's interest will turn to frustration, then pure and simple boredom: when is something going to happen?

You're in an interactive story: your player must have choices to make, and those that impose a trigger event are crucial for the adventure to continue. She must understand this well.

By no means leave her with choices concerning incidents, or without any real consequences. Not being able to really act in a universe where nothing happens is rarely exciting.

Secondary trigger events

After this, there can be tertiary, quaternary, etc.

These secondary trigger events are also, inevitably, connected to points of no return, and they follow the same logic as the first trigger event. The player must understand that, in the face of what is happening, she has to make a new decision. If this time of even shows the player that she doesn't control everything, which generates frustration, it offers her unpredictability and a change in the plot. So, this is the kind of frustration we're after, the kind that makes the player want to keep going, the kind challenges the player.

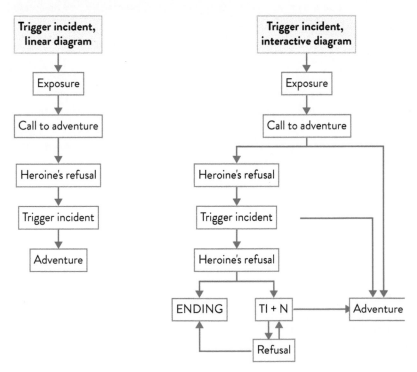

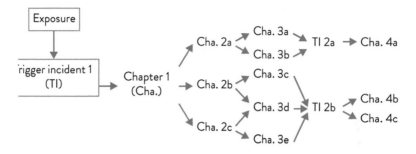

Trigger incidents, assets for controlling an interactive history.
Preventing a combinatorial explosion.

THE ART OF POINT OF VIEW AND REVELATIONS

Either you've already read the preceding parts about the universe and the characters, or you know all about the topic. But now you're interested in this more delicate aspect we know as point of view.

Indeed, now you have different elements to tell your story. You even have your main character or characters, secondary characters, and an idea of how to start this story.

But what angle are you going to tell it from?

This question will arise a lot because this is interactive script writing. From there, you have the leisure of change the points of view even more often than normal because you're going to write a story and its variants.

Ok, the main objective being interactive storytelling, the point of view will certainly be that of the main character. But will your player have an outside view, or will she have a subjective camera?

In the first case, she will physically see how her character behaves and his environment. In the second, she will only see the environment in her field of vision (if we exclude other information such as a touch screen, etc.), and she will not how her character physically interacts with the others. Often we only see the hands, the feet, or the arms, but not all the communications that is transmitted by facial expressions. If the character is a cold-blooded lizard, this will have but few consequences, but in humans, this isn't insignificant. And if your game is purely textual, will there also be a narrator or will your player have to content herself with what she can see of character in a few lines?

We'll make it clear already, the choice of point of view has big consequences on the game mechanics, its design, but also on the script writing.

If some things happen, let's say out of the character's field of vision but not the player's, you may turn the player into a spectator, so be very careful about this.

We have alluded that everything is generally played with the main character, but one can easily envisage the player playing one or two secondary characters for certain parts, certain missions. In and of itself, she'll play them like a main character, no matter.

The main issue that these gameplay choices raise is, ultimately, their influence on the revelations.

Thomas, how does the staging give information to the player to help the player make decisions?

Thomas Veauclin: Staging is a point of view. By nature, it's subjective. It inherently directs the player. Looking at all the cinema codes established over the years, it's easy to understand how to use it to achieve a purpose.

But staging is not just a tool like any other. One can easily make a purely narrative-based game without any staging at all.

What is a revelation?

First of all, what's going to weave and unravel your plot, not to mention your plots to your interactive narrative. A revelation can tie a story together (discovery of a new victim, the enemy base is empty, etc.) or unravel it (your teammate was an undercover FBI agent and is calling the calvary, the negotiations have forced the enemy to clear out). It is tied to your story. And, more particularly, it explains it or complicates its. A revelation can be tied to a trigger event, but it's not a rule. It often explains a trigger event after it has happened, but a trigger event is independent. You character could lose his family in a car accident. This could be a trigger event. Later, he learns that the mafia sabotaged the car. That's the revelation.

Revelations help you understand the story. They lead the player to continue the adventure. But since we're in an interactive story, it's up to you to decide which revelations are essential to achieving your story's aims and which ones are optional. You cannot do this in other types of stories. There's a revelation for such and such a thing, but you put it in or you don't. This is the luxury of an interactive story: the different branches can lead to different revelations.

Be careful: revelations with no connection to the plot are just information, and you mustn't overwhelm the player. You aren't there to show that you know how to write a story and universe, rather at the end of the game, the player should say to herself that this story wasn't bad at all, that what she lived in this universe was worth the time dedicated to it.

The art of revelations

This is about what the character discovers and what the player discover, which isn't necessarily the same thing. There are several possible cases, and you need to determine what they are so you know how to place the revelations. Because revelations are no more and no less than the story you're giving to the player. Without revelations, you might as well write a story where the player wanders around a labyrinth and has to get out. Period.

Depending on the media you're preparing your story for, you'll need to think about the points of view, but there is little difference. Indeed, you'll see that we talk about off camera sequences. It really doesn't matter if it's visual or auditory, the way the story is told is what counts.

The character and the player are connected

In this precise case, let's assume something extreme, the character has amnesia, and let's say that everything is in subjective camera. The character and the player will discover the universe together, you haven't planned any other point of view. The effect of surprise will be optimal. Next, depending on the choices offered, the player may miss more or less crucial information.

If you need to surprise the player, striking the right balance with revelations is more delicate in this mode. As everything is invariably coming without really any filter, you mustn't overload the player with information, but don't leave her desperately hungry for information either. We're already mentioned, frustration is a good element for motivating the player, but don't abuse it.

Revelations are tied to the story and the deployment of the plot. But this also concerns the universe you reveal, or the character's history. In the present case, if your player doesn't have a prolonged exploration phase (turning on a jukebox, browsing a book, etc.), she's going to be frustrated, in the bad sense of the term in interactive storytelling.

Careful, when we use the word "revelation," it is often associated with the Truth. But a revelation can also be used to mislead the player, simply because you present the truth from one angle, and she doesn't have all the pieces of the puzzle at the stage.

The narrator

Naturally, when you introduce another point of view, that's another entry point for information or revelations.

The narrator can be anonymous and, naturally, learning his identity will be the object of revelation – if he's anonymous from the start, the reason may be related to your story.

If the narrator's identity is known, there needs to be an explanation (Jules Verne tells the story, the old general remembers this war). It is often interesting to prepare a revelation concerning the narrator (he's really the man who executed your girlfriend with a boomerang, he's really a descendant of the people you saved, etc.)

The narrator is a secondary character, who narrates what happens to you as the main character (shall we introduce you to Doctor Watson?). Thus, he's well placed to reveal something about the story at a given time.

The narrator is the main character (like the voice-over of a private detective in a film noir), and, unless he's telling his story as a flash back while the player relives it, it is rare for the narrator to accompany the player up to the present, where there is no sequence dedicated to the narrator except the one in which the player is playing. The narrator can lie... Which can also lead to revelations.

Careful, the narrator turns the player into a spectator. Whether he allows you to make an ellipsis to transition from one scene to another, or to introduce a flash back, it doesn't matter, the player becomes a spectator. So, don't go overboard. It's generally agreed on, it's often a short clip or interlude.

Don't forget that in interactive storytelling, every time the narrator intervenes and turns the player into a spectator, it must not contradict the player's previous choices. This still obeys one simple word: coherence.

So, you will be truly be forced to plan several versions.

Off camera

What we refer to as off camera, here, is what the main character does not see, but the player does. For example, if you link it with a narrator sequence, this is the case if the narrator is not the main character.

You can very well plan sequences showing the big villain taking action, your wife or husband cheating on you with your best friend, etc.

Revealing the plot to the player in this way is quite basic. Or, it needs to be the very object of the game: you see how the killer did it, but now you have to figure out a way to interrogate him.

A subtler way, which should be used more parsimoniously, is to generate a false revelation. The player watches a scene that's going to make her think... But the outcome won't be as expected.

This isn't the coolest trick in the book, but remember we're writing an interactive story. To avoid going mad creating our arborescence, you need a technical storywriting solution. The player wants to live an experience she enjoys. She's not there to bestow you a posthumous Oscar for being the greatest scriptwriter of all time, especially if all your hard work behind the scenes doesn't cut the mustard on screen. Sometimes, you need to content yourself with being efficient.

You can also introduce a secondary character in this fashion. Now, concretely, you're not making a revelation concerning the resolution of the plot, but you're giving this character some extra appeal when the player meets him, or when she plays as this character, if you foresee this possibility.

Sequences with off-camera revelations are to be used with caution because your player becomes a spectator. Using them to make revelations about the universe is more prudent than for making revelations about the plot.

The mystery camera

You need a good reason to use this, but as you've read concerning other cases, the rules is always the same: the point of view is chosen to serve how you tell the story, how your reveal it.

So, if your player sees the main character from a strange angle, she will undoubtedly learn who is observing him, why and how. Otherwise, revise your framing and avoid making your player nauseous.

The player knows more than the character

To summarize, with the exception of the first case where the player is truly connected to the main character, she will learn more than the character; in and of itself, this isn't bad, the story is written for her, not for him. The player's advantage in this respect often helps reveal the universe, the past of the characters, all the these little things, more than we would ever be able to in other types of storytelling. On the other hand, always make sure that revelations moving the plot along are revelations for your player and her character. If you make, as we've already mentioned, revelations about something else, you'd better have a good reason because the player will become a spectator.

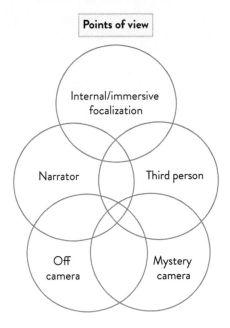

11. DIALOGUE

As you know, writing a story requires writing lots of other things beside the story itself, the universe, the characters' past, the trigger events, the point of view, how to reveal the story, etc.

Concerning this last aspect, we begin to get inside the writing and see what the player is going to experience. So far, you've see everything that's going to fill out the game, but what about the story itself, its arborescence, its graph? There isn't always something concrete.

So, you need to continue refining, but we're almost there. Your main character, your player, is going to talk, to act. This obviously can't be insignificant.

We'll talk about dialogue in the singular and the plural indistinctly.

THE CHARACTER DOESN'T SPEAK

Yes, you can be a tease when you really want to. You can decide on a story where the heroine, or all the characters do not speak. In a certain way, this will make things easier; dialogues don't have to be written; on the other hand, you deprive yourself of an advantage and, if we dare say, a joy of our trade: dialogues.

But let's come back to your character. First, just because he doesn't speak doesn't mean he doesn't communicate. You can use a caveman language to communicate by grunting and yelling.

Don't forget that, for any type of original, atypical or totally nutty communication, you'll need to include a learning period for the player to get the basics. The difficulty will be: turning a handicap into an advantage, something of interest. The player will undoubtedly understand very quickly which yell attracts a dozen tyrannosaurus rexes in heat, and which one makes the other dinosaurs flee. If you choose an original mode of communication, it must be connected with the story and the universe; again, you mustn't make something original for the sake of being original.

So, your character doesn't speak at all and does communicate with any sound, facial gestures, or expression? The fact may be you have a good reason, but, after all, if you're playing a tank, it doesn't much matter if it can laugh or cry. If you deprive yourself of the gold mine of interactivity that dialogues provide or, at the very least, communication, be sure of what you're going, or ask yourself whether the project is really right for you. If you're happy to write a story to play as a soulless robot that wanders around a manor in search of cans of oil, all much the better for you. You can skip this chapter on dialogue, if you haven't already. We note that, in this case, you are not supposed to read these lines, and this message, which is intended for you, will never be delivered to you. When we say coherence, it's a magic word.

AN ORIGINAL LANGUAGE

Or an original method of communication, at least.

Don't forget that if you create a language for your universe, or a mode of communication, this must represent a fun challenge for the player, not a long sigh in front of grammar and syntax files. Many will make an effort to make speaking elvish in Tolkien's universe, or Klingon in Star Trek, enjoyable. Otherwise, it's risky.

Nevertheless, with video games, the player is in control of her game time, and it can be unfortunate that working on language, or creating a language, is almost excluvisely based on a recurring theme = English is the language of the global market. First, if a lot of players make the effort to play in English, why wouldn't they make an effort to play in a new language?

The market is more limited, but neglecting the players' curiosity, their wishes, their taste for exploration, is often a way to cut off so many initiatives or bold innovations that the products that come out continuously all resemble each other "because that's what works."

Let's pursue the idea of dead or unusual languages, for a second. You can add a little extra something to your universe and characters by using other languages, though not necessarily for all of your dialogues. Obviously, you can't just say nonsense, and you need to have the right person to provide a good translation, but human thought is conveyed in great part through language, and you can do some amazing things with it. And don't forget, especially if you are writing a story involving a period in history, that all languages have older versions and that, often words have evolved, including words that have changed meaning or disappeared.

In this respect, neologisms are common in science fiction to describe what doesn't exist – be careful not to overload the player with too many neologisms. Either you tell her from the get go that she'll need to learn another language, or you methodically insert the new terms to avoid artificial dialogues where she won't understand anything.

The words should unlock the imagination, not hinder it.

THE MAIN CHARACTER SPEAKS

Or, at least, communicates.

And to avoid being redundant, what you read here also applies to secondary characters. A character's dialogue defines him. A warrior sure of himself would certainly not stumble over his words, however a shy student would undoubtedly stutter in public. For dialogues, carefully consider how you've characterized you characters: this needs to be coherent.

If we come back to the sure warrior, if he comes from nobility, he may ultimately have more have more manners, even if being a man of action leads him to be more blunt. On the battlefield, everyone sees right away whether you're a coward or not, you can't hide behind words. Maybe your shy student stutters in public, but uses a very rich vocabulary in his private circle of friends.

This coherence between the characters' profile and how they express themselves is fundamental. We will be more demanding with the main character and the secondary characters, but extras aren't to be neglected.

In many video games, now, it's common to hear the guards of place talk about there life, when they don't realize the heroine is spying on them. But for extras, more than anything, dialogues serve to set the tone of the universe.

And where's the player in all this?

In an interactive story, the benefit of having a character who speaks or communicates is that it allows the player herself to choose how her character expresses himself. So, for the main character, depending on the game objective, you have the possibility to offer the player different levels or tonalities of language.

Thus, she can be vulgar, laconic, ironic, etc.

It's up to you to determine whether it's an advantage for the gameplay and the story. Very concretely, what the main character says often has a strong influence on the relationships with the other characters.

In sum, the dialogues are going to give you a lot of work. Whether they are text-based or audio, you must always be attentive to what characterizes the main character and how you can offer the player different lines. And with all that, you need to weigh the consequences of the different lines.

The dialogues in interactive stories are much more work than normal. Really?

You'll see with the interactivity's mechanics, depending on the lines you offer the player, you can mislead her, or guide her choice. So, you need to be careful, too, not to slip in any unintended hints or guidance. The character's dialogues must be what the player wants to express.

THE PERSONALIZATION OF DIALOGUES

By this, we mean to focus on the main character and this character's relationship with the dialogue. The player speaks through the main character. If your main character has amnesia, then you can offer a wide variety of lines, even lines that completely contradict each other from one situation to another. Since the character doesn't remember, as opposed to the main player, what he says can vary greatly.

On the other hand, if you are playing a cop from the '70s nearing retirement whose ideas on everything are cut and dry, the character is well defined: the dialogues need to fit his character traits. The differences will be more subtle. It will be enjoyable for the player to see personalized dialogues relating, not to her, but to her character.

In the first extreme case (the amnesiac), the player expresses herself with the tone that she wants, the language she wants, and its her job to give her heroine a personality or not, by always responding bluntly, pleasantly, etc. In the second case, it's the character's personality that takes priority. The player can be blunt or pleasant, but each line will have a curse word, a suggestive remark, etc.

All this concerns human characters: if, in your story, the characters are very different, you may be forced to think about all this differently. That said, what is often pleasant, interesting, or even sought-after is to anthropomorphize things: making things act and talk like humans, whether your character be cats, Jupiterians, Norman wardrobes, etc. On the other hand, there's not escaping it, you'll have to stereotype their dialogues, otherwise it won't work. Your cats will be surprised to say "Catnabit!" the Jupiterians will curse, "By the rings of Saturn!" and your Norman wardrobes will often hesitate between "Perhaps maybe yes, perhaps maybe no..."

WHAT ARE DIALOGUES GOOD FOR?

Your dialogues need to fit with what you want to do with your characters, according to how you defined them.

But as Stendhal said, "Speech was given to man to conceal his thoughts."

The characters, including the player, can lie. As you just saw, dialogues are very useful for generating relationships with the other characters, and we can tell you, lying often come into play: lying knowingly, lying by omission, lying to protect someone, etc.

Conversely, choosing dialogues to convince someone else isn't any easier. The other humans function based on emotion and reason, the choice of words and tone of voice used by the player cannot be insignificant.

Whether it's to make a threat or seduce someone, your dialogues need to sound real, even if it's to lie.

If you're writing a strictly audio-based or text-based interactive story, without any visuals, then don't forget a fundamental element of dialogues: their purpose is to show things. Rather than using a narrator to describe a room, scene, etc., describe them using the characters. "The staircase is draining me, but I'll get to the top soon." What you want to avoid, if you have visuals, is exaggerating. If we say a character tiring as he climbs a staircase, there's no need to have him say that he's getting tired. That being said, there are always exceptions, particularly if that's part of the character's persona.

DIALOGUES, A SECOND WIND

Writing dialogues is a special moment between the author and the actors, from the moment your media calls upon the actors. So, write for the ones you like. Generally, this is how you write your best dialogues. Plus, by precisely imagining an actor, each character will behave differently. A dialogue is a pacing game. The meaning, as Michel Audiard used to say, is not the most important thing.

Don't stare at blank page. The point of departure is of little importance. What counts is the energy to carve our your scene and put the conflict in relief. The goal of the dialogue isn't to explain your story, rather to take it some place else. Your characters can bring a new facet about themselves or about others, too. They can get carried away, confide in each other, remember, etc.

Raising the stakes higher and higher is possible thanks to dialogue. Don't hesitate to magnify the behaviors, the characters, the egos, the dreams and the nightmares.

A character has never said his last word...

Devour films in your native language. Let yourself be taken by the dialogue. The advantage for human beings is that we reproduce what we see. So why not just watch masterpieces?

For actors, the notion of the character is sometimes vague. How does one create one? Why am I not simply the character? This concept exists for some people, hinders others, and for others, the concept doesn't even exist. No character, the actors bring everything to them.

No fear. On one hand, you can choose actors who are real characters. And next, imagine where they've never gone before. What could surprise them or amuse them so that they'll join your project? On the other hand, you can call upon chameleon actors, the masters of disguise.

Whether they are famous or not, the arrival of actors is a good sign. This probably means you've finished the structure. And this is where you'll need a second wind to go (back) over your dialogues.

So, do yo need to write the dialogues and find the actors or do you need to write specifically for the actors? The second option is more than appealing; if it's not already the case, try it out in moderation. In any case, it is always useful to organize readings to get familiarized with their diction, their huskiness and their preferred register. The comfortable they are with your work, the faster the filming or recording will go.

In addition, if you have a visual aid – whether a 2D or 3D illustration, or real clip – this is a blessing. The pictures provide information about the story. Take care not to repeat the same thing in the dialogues. On the other hand, the less help the pictures provide (extreme example: audio games), the more important the dialogues will be.

Many authors prefer to write dialogues in a peaceful environment, without music. Why? With Beethoven in the background, your dialogue may seem superpowerful. In the end, don't forget to reread your dialogues out loud to check whether they groove!

What's more, if we had to choose an aspect of the famous "Grand Theft Auto" series to talk about, it's probably this. Well yes, the quest to rise up the ranks is a success. Yes, the open world is impressive. Yes, having 5 stars and escaping the police takes more time than the story.

All things being equal, however, the dialogue is what gives the game its flavor. An open world means you need to grab your car and go from point A to point B. And this is *Rockstar*'s talent: using this constraint to shower us with exquisite dialogues. The characters have the time to express all their immorality and, in this game, the unforgettable Trevor, from episode V, continues to blow us away.

Before we conclude, don't forget to carry a notepad when you go for a walk. There are only ideas that count, and there are lines that hit the nail on the head! Speaking of which, here are some films with thunderous dialogues:

- *A Monkey in Winter* by H. Verneuil & *Under Suspicion* by C. Miller, dialogue by M. Audiard.
- *12 Angry Men* and *Dog Day Afternoon* directed S. Lumet.

Theater is also chock full of nuggets that are regularly adapted to film, such as *Glen Garry Glen Ross* by D. Mamet or *Sleuth* by A. Shaffer.

DIALOGUES DEPENDING ON THE MEDIA

We won't speak about this subject at length, but the media obviously limits your dialogues.

For comic books

In a comic book (manga, graphic novel, etc.) most of the time, they will be concise, but you can very well put in some extended dialogue. Just one thing, though, is it helpful?

And especially, unless you're making this a personal choice or an artistic statement, your dialogues mustn't describe what's illustrated in the same box or strip. We are not at the very beginning of when illustration all began. Your dialogues have meaning for the story, they compliment (i.e. created a contrasting effect) the illustration, but avoid describing the illustration.

And also plan for the when the player will make choices. You'll have very little space for long dialogues.

For choose-your-own-adventure books

In a novel, the dialogue can have a place for choices: you fully decide what you need based on your story, your characters. However, here, you're not writing a novel, but an interactive book. If your player spends her time reading dialogues where she has no choice, there's no longer any interactivity. However, making her choose her responses, if this continually involves a long dialogue, this is going to be painful, and you're going to multiply the paragraphs. It'll be so inflated. You can consider one page without a choice to be long, not out of the question, but long. So, if you enjoy dialogues where the player can choose what she wants to say, you may have an excellent arborescence, a great moment of one-liners and comebacks, but remember the player isn't going to play everything, so her game experience will be brief. However, in an interactive book, a choose-your-own-adventure book, there is a limited number of paragraphs and pages. The more you multiply the choices in the dialogues, the more you reduce the depth of your story and the game duration, be aware.

For roleplaying games

In a story for a roleplaying game, dialogues are rare, since the players are all going to play, and the gamemaster will play opposite them and vice versa.

You can plan dialogues for non-playing characters, secondary characters and extras, but in this case, focus on the key moments of the story – when, for example, a witness recounts what he has seen, when a king makes a speech, etc. If possible, you need a moment where the players, like their characters, are logically going to put themselves in a listening situation. Perhaps they'll interrupt the person speaking or make some jokes, but you can always resume from wherever you were at, or cut to another scene. We agree, this is more about monologues.

On the other hand, what might be practical for the person who's going to prepare your story for the player, and thus read it, is to prepare a question-answer meeting. You ask a question that the players are actually likely going to ask your secondary character, and you write the response in the form of a dialogue.

What was the butler doing last night? "I was organizing the bottles in the cellar, and then I thought..."

Do you want to write real dialogues where the characters interact with each other? This follows the same rules as before. This means the players will be in listening mode. For example, the husband and the wife argue in front of the wedding cake, while everyone was expecting a speech. Your players are hidden in the room and hear Cardinal Richelieu give orders to Rochefort, etc.

Dialogues are acted but most often improvised in roleplaying games, so you'll write little of them when doing an RPG story.

On the other hand, it is essential to give the gamemaster the character traits, the favorite expressions, the accent, etc., of the secondary characters. He must play them during the game. There will be many of them, and that's how he will produce the right dialogues to fit your story. That being said, if he feels a character in a different way, well he's the director, and you won't be there in any case to protest.

For the radio or a podcast, audio game, etc.

Do we have to state that dialogues are essential? And here, as it turns out, you can use rather long dialogues. In an interactive book, the player will always read the dialogues slower than an actor acting does. To put it simply, in the same amount of time, your actors will have exchanged more words than the reader will have read. Obviously, if she reads diagonally, she wins, but in this case, it's that she's undoubtedly replaying a choose-your-own adventure book.

For strictly audio, you'll have no other choice be to show the extent of your talent. Never forget the sound engineer. If your dialogues can serve you to describe what's happening, the places, by sliding in observations, a good sound engineer can help you focus on the acting of your actors, on the action, more than on the need to render the characters' environment visible.

A narrator certainly has a place in an audio story by reminding you that you can also make a commentator out of him. And, in addition, the narrator can address the player: "And now, what do you?"

For audiovisual

Do we need to remind you how important dialogues are in this type of media? As with comic books, avoid describing what's visible to the character. For the rest, since the dialogues are acted, you can have a bit of fun, but don't forget that your player must be able to make choices and not get the impression she's at the movie theater.

If she has the choices of many lines, don't forget that, in theory, you'll have to film each distinct reaction from the characters interacting with her – and that means time and money. A little like a choose-your-own adventure, an audiovisual story is, in short, a rather limited product. Not so much because of the size (nowadays we can store so much data), but because of the production. If you make an audiovisual game where the player plays a female version of Woody Allen, imagine the nightmare in terms of arborescence, and how long it would take to shoot.

So, enjoy yourself with the dialogues, but choice of lines for the player must have implications for the story. You will see in the part about choices that, while we're permitted to create them for the ambiance, the tone, etc. without them being crucial to the story, in audiovisual, you can rarely afford this luxury.

For a video game

Here, this will vary a lot. It all depends on the game you have planned and the technology. We're assuming that this book will especially help you with story-driven games more than platform games, etc. That being said, it all depends on how your dialogues are presented:

- As text: in this case, it's better to follow the rules of choose-your-own adventure books. The player mustn't have pages and pages to read before making a choice. On the other hand, you can easily cut the dialogue up into plenty of small choices to set the tone, the atmosphere, which won't change, when doing this, the ensuing dialogue of the secondary characters. Here, if you just have to load the text, just load the text, then you can let loose on the dialogue.

- Audio: this will, thus, follow the audiovisual rules, however it takes much less time and is less expensive to do some atmosphere dialogue, as explained below. It's often less complicated than re-shooting one variant of a scene with the actors. In this case, you can align some dialogue because you'll make the player intervene.

12. ACTION

There's more to life than dialogue, particularly if you can do many things you can't in the real world: teleporting, shooting fire balls, jumping on floating platforms, dodging exploding mushrooms, etc.

Sometimes, your characters will be content to search an area, or open a door, even though opening a door can often be moment of tension related to the game: what's going to jump out at you?

In a situation where you have spectators, and not players, the action is felt, experienced by empathy, but they don't have any means of action. Here, your spectator is a player. So, if she opens the door, it's her decision (or not), and she'll assume the consequences. Maybe the scriptwriter has forced her to do this.

Always remember to offer choices and to make the choices to the actions immediately visible to the player. This is possible with the dialogues; it is a certainty with the action.

Action has to be handled differently depending on the media.

FOR A COMIC BOOK

Action lends itself excellently to graphic interpretation. However, your comic book has a limited number of strips. And your illustrator, or your illustration team, will want to work on different pictures. If you're making an interactive comic book where the changes from one picture to another are subtle depending on the choices, you'll run out of space. This may sound biased (perhaps on a survey, for example), but what makes a comic book enjoyable are the pictures. By changing just one element of a picture, it can lessen the impact.

If you're make an interactive digital comic book, such as a visual novel, then you'll virtually have an unlimited number strips, and your illustrator, or illustration team, will be able to make small alterations to offer a significant number of small details based on the choices. Enjoying a comic book hinges on the artistic preference for the illustrations.

IN A CHOOSE-YOUR-OWN-ADVENTURE BOOK

You have to describe what the character can do and how the character does it. However, since it is still a game, you can just ask the player to roll dice and see if she rolls correctly. Describing the action in an interactive book is a choice of gameplay: must my player be able to read the result of her actions, whether positive or negative, in detail? Or, conversely, am I okay with indicating the result in the following paragraph? In an interactive book, the action is often divided into small pieces and spread out from paragraph to paragraph. If not, the action is a test or fight that must be won according to the game's rules, but most of the time, the result of the action leads to another paragraph.

Always try to have at least one small phrase relating to the tone of your story before sending the reader to another paragraph, or try to maintain a little tension, or a lot. Try to create a bit of suspense. The player shouldn't get the impression she's using an index to get to the right paragraph. And, well, most of your players will never have used an index, and no we're not talking about the finger.

So, you can resolve the action with the rules system, which can very well contain a description of the sequences (e.g. kick, type of shot, etc.), however the consequences must be described.

FOR ROLEPLAYING GAMES

And more precisely, roleplaying game story. The action, which doesn't necessarily have to be a fight, must be described so the gamemaster can direct the game, and it must describe the different consequences. The action will be resolved using the system provided by the game. This include a dozen rolls of the dice or verbal jousting.

As you see, the variety of game systems make it impossible for us to guide you on this technical aspect.

On the other hand, in a roleplaying game, the player clearly has more freedom, so plan for lots of lines for the consequences to the action. As a scriptwriter, it's hard for you to know how the action scene is going to turn out when the player is going to play it. Also, your attention will be focused on building your scene and its connection to the scenes before and after it.

The resolution of an action is the moment in an RPG game where anything can happen, so remain zen. In this web of possibilities, you must, above all, make sure your threads are solid and conducive. After that, if the characters slip through, the fall will be somewhat long.

FOR RADIO

This is almost identical to the previous chapter about dialogues. In radio, the dialogues are everything, and the sound engineer is your best friend.

For an action scene where the player can choose whatever she wants to do, remember that she can't see anything. So, her decisions will be made based on what you've provided in the audio. If a door squeaked, she can imagine someone came in, but if we only hear this door, it's going to be more difficult. In this way, you can play with the difficulty level, but take care not to force your player to have to play with the volume all the way up, sitting straight up in order to focus on every little detail.

However, since there is nothing to see, you have more leeway to offer different resolutions, or different consequences to choices, as long as the actor doesn't have to do a dozen variants. However, as stated at the beginning of this book, this isn't as much work and doesn't takes as much time as filming.

FOR AUDIOVISUAL

Since everything is acted out, this means an economy of means. You're writing an interactive story, so the more possible choices you give to your player for an action, the more you'll have to film. If there are several choices, it's likely you'll be asked whether some of them lead to the same result. Because of the costs in terms of time and money, interactivity is more limited in a media like audiovisual. As we mentioned at the beginning of this book, the constraints on filming need to be taken into consideration, especially in retroplanning.

FOR A VIDEO GAME

As we pointed out at the beginning of the book, we prefer text-based, story-driven video games. It's true that if you have a platform game, there is constant action and the player's choices are more about reflex and the ability to build a movement strategy in the game space.

That being said, as for dialogues, video games lend themselves to interactivity.

You may have a technical concerns: what's the game engine's capacity?

But you'll certainly be concerned with the gameplay. How do I not bore the player? Or, how do I not disorient her? The action must serve the story. After that, yes, a video game can allow you to juxtapose a platform scene, a shooting scene, a castle search scene, etc. We'll come back to what we underscored earlier: time management, i.e. managing your work time. You'll need to limit yourself, but with time management, the team working with you will manage to duplicate or add small variants without a problem. Your job will be to maintain the thread, the threads of your plots, to offer a story.

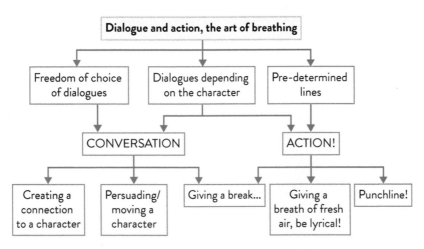

13. BUILDING A SCENE

Here we are, at this point we're beginning to have different elements, but for now, nothing concrete has been built.

More than anything, a good scene is a hallway. The main character needs to be seized by a string that pulls her to the next scene. This urgency is made possible by some deep motivations. What is propelling my character to act? And by a conflict with multiple fronts, in the scene and outside it. What is preventing her from acting? And how can she overcome this obstacle?

If your character's quest is solid and coherent, this is an excellent start. Each scene must, thus, bring her closer to her goal (or at least give her think so).

Imagine the developments in your story are placed on a spring. By alternating high pressure and low pressure scenes, you're going to keep your player's attention. If apply too much pressure, the spring breaks and, on the contrary, if you don't push hard enough, the player may get bored.

This book deals with interactive stories for different media. Each one has specific constraints, but, inevitably, they're going to tell a story, and this story can break down, especially in interactive fiction. One of the key elements is the scene.

SCENE CUTTING

As a general rule

We're going to use this phrase generically, since the objective is to help you with interactive scriptwriting across different media. So, yes, a scene for audiovisual or for audio (radio), it's obvious, and one can do this in acts. For roleplaying game stories, there's nothing preventing us from thinking in terms of scenes. On the other hand, let's see where this doesn't work, or at least where it's not so obvious.

For a comic book

In a comic book, the cutting has to do with the strip. In a linear comic book, you need a beginning and an end to the strip, and depending on its positioning in the book (even or odd page), there are some subtleties.

Unfortunately, in an interactive comic book, the interaction can make you jump from one box to another, and not necessarily in the same strip. So, when the scriptwriter thinks of the story, he has to think in terms of scenes, precisely because, later, they're ultimately going to be cut up and spread out, more or less.

Cutting up the comic book, however, really depends on the medium, so thinking carefully in terms of scenes is going to help you prepare your work. On the other hand, let's be clear, you will not have the same tension as with other mediums, the same climax, because you have to browse the comic book and this lessens the dramatic effects. In interactive comic books, the visual enjoyment and the enjoyment of playing are going to be greater than the narrative enjoyment. You may disagree, but this is our artistic point of view. The aesthetic emotion is stronger when you read a linear comic book compared to when you play an interactive comic book.

For choose-your-own-adventure book

A novel can be divided into chapters, but, again, that's a linear narrative. In an interactive book, your story is cut up and distributed into paragraphs. Thinking in terms of chapters makes things complex. Sure, we can tell ourselves that, in such part, such as an act, such or such thing is going to happen, but you can't line up the chapters. Rather, think in terms of scenes: an action scene, an interrogation scene, a voyage scene, etc. A scene can be cut up more easily.

However, this complicates the climax. Even if the player's choices lead to an increase or decrease in tension, or if they bring the plot together or unravel it, here, she's going from one paragraph to another. You can't expect to achieve the same effects. Like with interactive comic books, the emotions felt, the aesthetic emotion, won't be as strong in an interactive book as they are with a novel. On the other hand, the enjoyment of the game, which, in sum, is what a choose-your-own-adventure book is exactly aiming for, is quite real, and that's what you need to count on.

Your play is going from one paragraph to another. You can make the cutting more or less transparent. Nothing is preventing you from numbering acts or giving them titles, but the need to divide your story up into several stories, because of the game between the paragraphs, lessens the aesthetic emotion. Don't forget that, even by bouncing from one paragraph to another, we still need to surprise the player. And the surprise generates a strong emotion. We're putting you on notice. As opposed to a book, your player is going to live an adventure, based on her choices.

For a video game

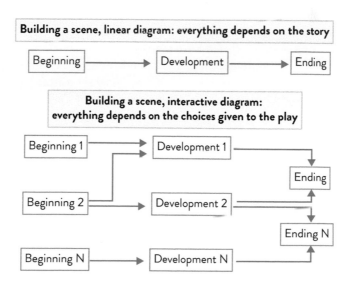

Building a scene, linear diagram: everything depends on the story

Beginning → Development → Ending

Building a scene, interactive diagram: everything depends on the choices given to the play

Beginning 1 → Development 1
Ending
Beginning 2 → Development 2
Ending N
Beginning N → Development N

Obviously, for narrative-based video games, you can and should think in terms of scenes – these games bring the story to the fore. For platform games, for example, if we look closely, each level can be considered to be a scene. You need to enter and exit, and if possible raise a challenge. Something is happening.

Because of their plasticity, video games lend themselves well to being cut up into scenes.

David, how do you control the pace of an interactive story if the player is the one in control of the story?

David Cage: The main challenge of an interactive story is the fact that it's not a story I'm not telling alone. I'm telling it with a partner: the player. I have to do my share of the work just like the player does in order to have the best experience possible. My job is to put forth a context ideal for interaction and interesting, profound and well-paced choices The player, for his part, has to play the character and be honest with the story.

The work we did on the pacing of *Detroit* for example is something interesting. We opted for shorter scenes, from 15-20 minutes, and think it's what we needed. You have the time to build up the situation, to tell a story and at the same time, it's short enough so the player doesn't get bored.

And you, Joe?

Joe Pinney: I think of the story a little a traditional linear story. Normally, I don't give too much control to the player over the dramatic intensity of the scene. The player controls the way he behaves and treats others. The player's choices must matter, but they generally matter more in the relationships among the characters than in the plot. This simultaneously allows you to minimize production costs and maximize emotional impact. In visual media, branches consisting of large parcels are expensive, so we save them for moments or choices that really matter. Personalizing the character relationships is a relatively good deal, and it creates strong emotional connections. This is where the magic is. When the player cares about the other characters in the story, the interactive narrative can take them places that no other art form can reach.

FibreTigre, how to you manage the pacing in your interactive writings?

FibreTigre: You have to write in great detail. A long, contemplative introduction, a quick, very dense interactive action sequence, a lengthy narrative bottleneck, an action sequence, etc. The amount of text must give the pacing to the action, in addition to words and punctuation.

INTRODUCING CHARACTERS

Here we're focusing on introducing characters, not just in scene, but in the game. They're all going to appear for a first time, in the same scene or in different scenes. We'll be looking at the extras abstractly. On the other hand, all the characters you've worked hard on deserve to enter the came in a notable way, if not unforgettable.

This depends a lot on the tone, the atmosphere and your personal choices before they become the player's choices.

It may seem logical to introduce the main character's team to him if he's a police officer. But this can be in a scene at the police station, or each time he needs a specialist.

In an interactive story, you can tie character introductions to the game's mechanics: until a player meets a certain condition, she doesn't get to meet a certain character. You can even make goals with them. It's quite common in video games to have to go to a certain place or obtain such or such thing before you can meet a certain boss, face him or meet a certain important character, to obtain his support, or information.

You can also introduce characters in short cinematic scenes where the player momentarily becomes a spectator. Few players will hold it against you. And as we've already mentioned, in your project it's possible to have the player play secondary characters, which is a very immersive way of introducing them.

What you need to remember is that the characters you develop, when you have need of them for a scene and it's their first appearance, you need to give them some attention. It's their moment of glory. After that, for better or worse, they're there to make the player look good. It's kind of harsh to put it that way, but this is meant to encourage you to give them the spotlight at least once.

There are four main thematic ways of introducing characters.

- **In media res.** The player is thrust into the action and must make choices right away. This is a proven method for starting an adventure and introducing the main character. And if there are secondary characters, you can introduce them later, give them your attention in a flashback, or when they finally have time, once they're safe, you can let them catch their breath and talk to the player.

- **Hop o' My Thumb.** This will be more of a "Retro Hop o' My Thumb." Your player is going to gradually discover the secondary characters you've spread throughout the plot. So, each character will have its own introduction. And often one character will have spoken of the next one, to give her an idea (false or justified) of what awaits her.

- **Recruitment.** Your character has to put a team together, so you'll need to look after your dossiers.

- **Into the unknown!** Your character doesn't know what to expect in this universe. This is often the time to have some fun and mix things up by making an explosive or jarring introduction, you choose.

And the main character? Introducing the main character is a particular case because she's tied to the start of the adventure. We'll come back to this.

NO CLIMAX, NO SCENE

This famous fermata that is the climax, even if the formula is a little outdated, everyone will tell you to work on it. Your scene hinges on it. It raises the tension, which draws the player in all the while developing your story.

So, yes, a climax often appears more than once in a story. Whether you group your scenes in sequences, in acts, it matters little, you're going to need climaxes. If not, this means that parts of your story are not interesting at all. This is a rather severe judgment, and all the more so given that this is an interactive story.

Actually, depending on your project, why not have some useless scenes? This may seem like an aberration, and a waste of time and money, but if you really want it that way, go for it. If you accumulate them, only then is the player quite likely to keep playing.

Attention, however, a useless scene has nothing to do with an exploration scene, a scene intended to set an atmosphere. In interactivity, you benefit more anyway from more exposure time to introduce things than in a burdensome filmed scene.

Digging the conflict

Get a shovel, it's time to dig. We promise, if you dig deep, you'll hit black gold.

Attention, the conflict isn't about suffering! The main character doesn't suffer. He goes out of his way to preserve his dignity. Among the players, only a few are interested in a character who suffers or whom we feel sorry for. What inspires us is his courage, his outrage, his freedom. You character is not a victim. He's responsible for his acts. The conflict isn't about one act of physical violence after another either.

Call of Duty isn't just a shoot 'em up. It's an ideological game where values clash. *Wolf Among Us* isn't just a quest game. It's a reflection on the sense of duty and justice.

The conflict consists of seeing convictions, values, principles clash. This is how you'll offer the player the most difficult dilemmas to resolve. You player is torn between two convictions (inner conflict) and doesn't know which one to choose. In general, the dilemma, according to Corneille, pits duty against love. A (re) read of *Le Cid* can provide more insight on the notion of choice.

No to useless scenes

We aren't certain, but it's better to write it in black and white.

How can one distinguish between a useless scene and an exploration, exposure or other kind of scene? A useless scene, if you cut it, the story only gets better. That's the test. The other scenes, if you cut them, something is missing: an, the tone is all of a sudden too harsh, the ellipsis loses the player, etc.

We've mentioned it before in this book, proofreading and having someone proofread is a good way to detect this kind of scene. Sometimes, you try to put too much in, or, more often in interactive script writing, an element has change in the story, and the scene is now out of place. However, we cannot repeat it enough, you're writing an interactive story with numerous branches. As soon as you modify one thing, this may impact another point in the story, and this very detail can escape you, simply because a narrative with multiple choices is a job that requires permanent memory.

Yes, your useless scene may very well have the best climax of the year. In this case, if you don't want to waste this effect, it's up to you to see if you can rework it. Bear in mind that, if it's difficult to abandon a good idea, perhaps it will it will fit in another story better than the one you're currently writing.

It may reassure you to know that authors are often astonished by their own ability to remember that changing this or that will have such or such repercussion.

This is a good thing. But they always make a point to proofread and check. This is even better.

If you're really stuck on a story, here's a tip: delete the scene you care about the most. When we say *stuck*, this means a real problem that the proofreadings haven't been able to resolve. It's sometimes cruel, but when you try to put a big round peg in a square hole, it gets stuck. This scene you care so much about may be the reason the reason your structure is so fragile. And maybe this scene is better used elsewhere; at best for another branch, at worst for another story.

Placing the climax

You can also place several of them. There's nothing preventing you from building it up in stages in your scene. However, the higher you go, the more you'll have to sort things out to land back on your feet.

A scene consists of an introduction, a development and a conclusion.

Unity of time, place and action? This is a frequent constraint in theater, but we're not doing theater. That being said, it's a good way to keep yourself from getting lost and to build a strong scene. There are proven methods, and this is part of them. So, you can go ahead and say that your scenes have to be, for example, in real time, in each room of the manor, and each time, we discover something a new element of the plot. It's not as easy as that.

Or, your scene could very well begin on the docks in New York and finish in Central Park. This would be a typical chase scene. Note that, in this case, you have your unity of place with New York, but ok, one can imagine some sci-fi stories with a chase scene from dimension to dimension through portals, and, well now, here the unity of place becomes a very abstract notion...

A beginning and an ending

The example of a chase is very good for this because one can easily see the beginning and the ending. There is action throughout the chase. The time for a chase scene is generally brief, but in cinema, for example, some chases scenes are never ending, or even reach cult status (we're thinking of *Blues Brothers*, among others).

What matters is that we know we're moving on to another element of the story: your scene begins. From here, the starting point, it's the start of your chase, the meeting with the witness, the arrival on the soccer field, etc., you need to about your climax, your culminating point. You're going to put some obstacles in your chase, and they can be increasingly difficult or, if you're in the street, they can be random, but at some point you need to mark this point. In your soccer match, you look at the climax as an intense moment in the match. In the testimony of your witness, a series of revelations, seduction and intimidation leads to the climax.

Feeling the climax

It's not about adding variables and telling yourself that the climax arrives with a certain score. This is the problem with climaxes. It's an artistic notion. Some things are obvious: opening a drawer is not a climax. Putting a cut off hand inside, ok you're getting closer – if your detectives are looking for a clue. Or an arguing couple reaches its culminating point and, whoop, the husband slips and falls down the staircase. Or, less gruesome, the character opens his mail and reads a dismissal letter while he's talking to his partner about the future.

Presented like that, your climax often resembles a revelation. Why? You have to move the story forward, and, in addition, you, you manage different stories in your interactive script. Generally, suspense precedes your climax, so it's beneficial to place a revelation there.

In pure action scenes, where there's a fight or a shootout (and quite often both), you can often make the character have a brush with death, and in interactive storytelling, quite often the player will be the one who's responsible for the character's survival, or not. This type of scene is less suitable for a revelation, but this could be the shooter's identity, once neutralized, a clue the enemy left behind while fleeing, etc.

So, yes, coupling the climax with a revelation easily announces the end of a scene. Note that you can have multiple climaxes to make the impact and, in this case, the revelation bigger; for example, as each drawer is opened, another part of a human body is discovered. There was a murder, and, because of the dismemberment and the gruesome staging, the murder is all the more cruel. Or the witness reveals increasingly disturbing information. Or your heroine, who wants to escape a dungeon, kills a horror more terrifying than the previous one in each new room as she gets closer to the exit.

You notice a climax, you feel the tension and the suspense in the scene.

Of course, you don't have to string together bloody clue or fight scenes. There's nothing stopping you from stringing together gags or more and more improbable things leading to slapstick. That said, stringing together gags is far from easy. Which brings us to the next point.

Scene pacing

In a chase, it's easy to understand that everything has to come together quickly. But in an interrogation, this can play out more slowly. Even your action scenes, especially if you're in an story-based interactive video game, can have very different pacings, depending on whether the player can play her character in slow motion, whether she can pause the game to think about her next action, or whether she has to react by reflex rather than act, etc. Think carefully about being on point with the gameplay and the game mechanics. On paper, they look all perfect, but when it comes to playing them, things can get out of control.

Bearing that in mind, remember that your scene needs pacing. The faster the pace, the more implausible things you can do, and the more you can suddenly raise the tension. The slower the pacing, the more you play on the atmosphere, on a mounting suspense that crescendos – but be careful of getting too far fetched.

The more time the player has to explore, to settle in, and to observe, the tighter your story should be, otherwise she may discover inconsistencies, or things of this nature. Because the player is building her story based on her journey but also based on her own imagination; true, she follows your branches, but it's not a red herring. Her memory, builds gradually her story. Bear this well in mind when pacing your scenes: if the player can come to an intersection in different ways in your story, and this scene has particular pacing, this pacing may contrast with what your player just experienced on a particular path.

To maintain good pacing, there's no other choice but proofreading and testing.

INTRODUCING THE GAME

This is a particular scene.

You can precede it with a cold open, or a prologue where the player is a spectator or where she can interact. She can even interact by playing as a character other than the heroine. The object of a cold open is to prepare the player and give her some information (story objectives, tone, atmosphere).

A cold open where you can play (including the victim of the serial killer or a marine before disembarking) also allows you to feel out the playing system, allowing the player to try it out. And it's too bad if this doesn't go off well because, as it is, the introduction character's fate is sealed, for better or for worse. This merges with the interactivity mechanics.

You main character may not be introduced during the cold open, but we can eventually start to talk about him. Depending on the media you have in mind, you might not be able to include this scene, but a book can have a prologue, just like a comic book. Ultimately, you're the author. See what's good for the story and the player.

Next comes the introduction scene. This can including anything from your player being hired, commissioned, or recruited for a mission to a character who opens his eyes in a dimly lit cave.

Your introduction scene is going to set the tone for your game, at least the first act. Everything depends on whether you've planned any twists (different from switches) or rather different adventures based on the branches.

If you have already read parts of the book, you'll notice that we talk about genres often. These can help you. Genres often have typical introductions, which you'll need to customize to give them a certain appeal. You can choose a run-of-the-mill introduction if you suddenly turn the universe's codes upside down and throw things off balance. But if you do a run-of-the-mill introduction and load it with clichés, your story won't take off or, too late, the player will have stopped playing.

Whether your introduction is an homage to fantasy or never-before-seen erotica, the objective is to make your player want to continue. This isn't necessarily about making a trailer with explosions everywhere, it's about creating expectation. A disturbing forest at night, with a strange breathing sound in the background, will also get the job done for an investigation, for horror, etc. As always, the key word is coherence.

You can dupe the player from the start, make her believe what you want. During the introduction, she appears in your story, and the introduction is going to be her starting point for building her own adventure herself. So, you can slide in some gifts or some voodoo dolls from the start, it all depends on your project and your gameplay.

Remember that you're writing an interactive story. Consequently, the purpose of your introduction scene isn't just to start the adventure: you have to play.

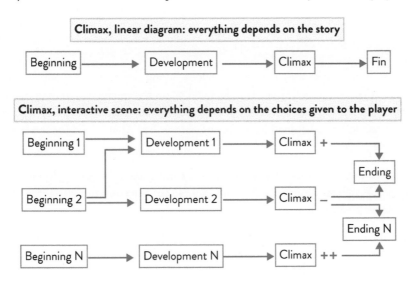

PRO INSIGHT

How does one manage the pacing of a story with an interactive narrative, since ultimately it's in the players hands?

Jean-Luc Cano: Indeed, one really doesn't have control. In interacting storytelling, a lot of things have to be considered: like the puzzle, the game design, etc. The scrip writer really only has control over little bits of a scene. It's up to him to give the appearance of pacing. I write each scene as if it were a TV episode and try to pace theme as much as possible. But, ultimately, in a video game, the pacing isn't the most important thing because it's the player who decides.

Thomas Veauclin: You put different gameplay phases and their estimated times on paper, and that let's you easily see whether you have an imbalance in terms of pacing. You always have free phrases and some written phases. You can't estimate free phases. It all depends on what the player does. So, it matters little. You know what is accessible for the player at the point, and the time doesn't matter much.

If you ask someone to go from point A to point B, all you have to do is calculate the time it takes to get there. That's your minimum time. If some players prefer to go get lost elsewhere, that's their choice, but they're doing some off-piste stuff. That's perfect, it's not a big deal, but you can't guarantee the pace, so you don't worry about it anymore.

But since this the player chose to go off piste, this won't frustrate him. When he feels like, he'll just go to point B, and, here, you get him back.

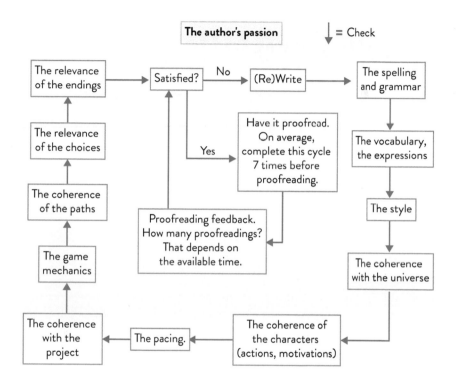

PART 4

THE MECHANICS
OF INTERACTIVITY

Interactivity is not only a matter of technological power, more than anything it's a conceptual methodology that allows you to offer the player a truly personalized, emotional simulation.

Armed with the right tool in the form of arborescence, you make your experience bigger by offering the sentiment that your universe is one of infinite possibilities. The anticipation and constant exploration of an interactive story are made possible by numerous mechanics that can easily be combined.

14. MASTERING THE WORK TOOLS

MASTERING THE LANGUAGE

This may seem obvious, even insulting, but it's the truth: we can't write stories unless we master the language they're made with. Indeed, if you tell a story, oral expression may spare you numerous constraints that apply to written language because, particularly with French, there are numerous things we can't hear, and your mistake, your error, won't be noticed. Yet, should you sabotage your dialogues for this reason?

Even if, in spoken, written or narrated language, you can twist the language, there is no grammar or spelling, there is syntax: if your sentence doesn't mean anything, it doesn't mean anything, whether your sing it or have your player read it.

You're writing a story. An interactive story can't break the rules of the language you're writing in.

Always remember that when reading a novel, a story, a paragraph, or a text, if your reader notices a mistake, that's going to break the rhythm, ruin the story, take the reader out her imagination, where she had immersed herself. A mistake, typo or error sends her back to the present. I'm reading something in print, a digital text, I notice a mistake. Your player will also detach from the story, from the tension, the suspense, the pace, you've sabotaged your work with mistakes.

And don't even come to us and say, "It's no big deal, it's just a game." We're doing something the right way, and if you believe your audience has less mastery of language than you, then tell yourself that it's your duty to present them with a product done right; you're writing, so you're setting an example. No one expects a plumber to say a leak is no big deal. No one wants a leak. Period.

Syntax and vocabulary are going to give meaning to your story because you master the language. Even if you're writing a simple preparatory work document, if no one understands it, then whats the point? True, it's ok to be more tolerant with a work document, often prepared in a short amount of time, but it does not bode well if you massacre Goethe, Moliere or Shakespeare – by the way, choose your victim in your native language. On this point, let's be clear, read translations to expose yourself to other cultures, to open your mind to new kinds of imagination.

And it's not just about showing that you're more talented than spell check.

Your language, your imagination

Everything was just technical, then a good word processor would suffice, and that would be it!

But the thing is, once you learn a language, and express yourself in a language, you think in it. And you feed your imagination with it. So, by not developing a mastery of your language, you handicap yourself when you want to use your imagination. Read books, watch films, play, go to exhibitions, culture yourself, so that you feed your imagination.

However, if you, then, want to express your ideas in writing, you need to know how to write. If you express yourself by dancing, you cannot tolerate clumsy, maladroit movement, once you know the first steps.

It's not about knowing the basics of writing to write a story, you need to go beyond that, you need to work your language. If you've read, you've come across new words, you memorize them, you discover them, and above all you learn their meaning and their context of use. The richer and more precise your vocabulary, the more you can play on a wide array and deploy a deeper, more refined imagination. We are no longer on the idea of simply not making mistakes but rather enriching the world, embellishing it, or even better, re-enchanting it.

You write to make life extraordinary, to take your player out of the ordinary, to diminish the banality, to forget everyday life. The experience the player is going to live is going to enrich her own culture, develop her imagination.

And all that, that's work. In this book, you'll find some typos, some phrases we may have able to lighten up, some style we could have worked more, but the object isn't to take you somewhere else, to immerse your soul and plant a new seed of imagination.

But you, you're writing a story. Your responsibility is much greater. It's immense. Without imagination, humans don't invent anything; without that little thing that stimulates our curiosity, our intelligence, we're not going to see what lies beyond, whether it's behind a door, a hill or a solar system.

Take care of the vocabulary, the effects you want to give. You read about it in character creation. Characters can express themselves anyway and anyhow they want, but even if you write using slang in a text message, write well!

MASTERING WORD PROCESSING

Free office, Word, OpenOffice, etc. It doesn't matter which, just know how to use one. Not the least to master the presentation because, at a minimum, your proofreaders have to proof your writing, plus everyone else who works with you. If you deliver dense tomes without a title, without points of reference, without anything, it will be a disaster, you're giving them extra work. Everything that is done well from the start avoids useless back and forth; you gain time and efficiency.

You're writing an interactive script, not a novel, not a film. So, you'll need titles, etc. so the reader of your story can have reference points in your branches.

Lots of word processors allow you to put tags and browse with hypertext links in your document; don't hesitate to use them, especially if you're working on a text-based interactive narrative. In any case, this will already give a hint of inter-activity by helping the reader browse. And this also allows you to test a part of the story, even if all the gameplay is undoubtedly absent.

For word processing, never forget that the spell check knows what you're typing, not what you're thinking. It will always try to correct you according to the standard, but this may not be the effect you're going for, particularly in the dialogues. There has been a lot of progress, but don't make a correction without thinking. It still happens that some characters have a delicious "desert after they eat." So for pity's sake, be meticulous!

David, in your interactive story projects, how do you go about getting your teams started on production without them getting lost in the arborescence or the methods you use?

David Cage: I write as if I were writing a film script. I use a very specific type of grammar and framing, colors and a precise *template* to make reading as enjoyable and as clear as possible. It's difficult because you have to portray something that isn't linear; with a linear format, it's similar to a choose-your-own-adventure book.

I also provide my teams with tools, visuals and *concept art,* but also a full structure of the arborescence. I work with writing software to show the branches and visually portray the structure of each scene and the full game so that everyone can clearly visualize it as a whole.

One of the main challenges is actually to get your team inside your project because that's who's going to implement your work. So, it's imperative that your team understands each detail, each nuance. To do this, I work on the documents a lot, but I also spend time talking with the people involved, particularly before starting a scene in order to make sure everyone is on the same wavelength.

Joe, what interactive storytelling tools do you use?

Joe Pinney: I've used all sorts of tools, from proprietary flow-chartering software to Google docs. I learn better by immersing myself and trying to create something, and by asking my colleagues (or people online) stupid questions over and over.

Could you describe the multi-person writing process? Do you have a showrunner?

At Telltale, I've worked with a team of narrative designers and scriptwriters on each episode, including a showrunner normally responsible for making sure everything is coherent. Working with a creative team is great. You can inspire each other, improve each other's work and just laugh a little. Creative conflicts are inevitable, everyone must be able to listen and be open-minded. There is a limit to the number of people you can assign to a creative team to speed up development. At some point, you start to step on other people's feet, and adding people slows things down.

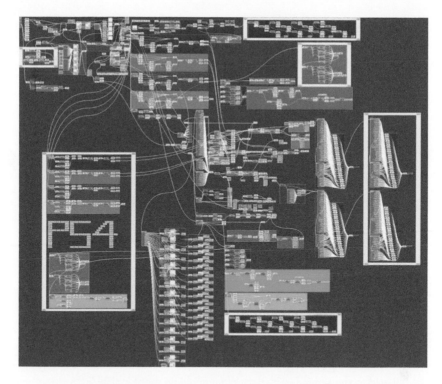

Quantic Dream's internal arborescence structure tool used to track production

INTERACTIVITY WITH TWINE

This free authoring software is well design for getting started in interactive script writing but also for proposing mock-ups to your clients.

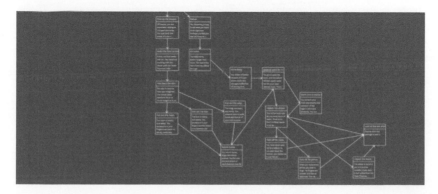

For beginners

First, Twine is free, and there is, at least as I write these lines, a community around this software.

We recommend you download version 1.4.2, rather than using the online version. To save your files, the downloadable version is preferable. An author likes to keep his files under his arm, not so much in the cloud.

All joking aside, since this part is for beginners: back up your work! We can't stress it enough, back up your work, and on different media (USB drive, cloud, external disk drive, etc.)!

Twine, you'll see, is a world of blocks connected by links, and little by little you create an arborescence.

The Twine community adds a lot of code to bolster its features, but at the start, stick with the basics: [[path 1]]. The link between square brackets is the key to Twine. You can type your text and add as many links to other blocks as you want, thanks to [[...]].

One of Twine's limits is the name of your links. Twine doesn't accept duplicates. Thus, if you have [[path 1]], you can't reuse it for a different block. Each [[path 1]] will lead to the same destination. What could be more logical?

Except that, if you have choices such as [[Open the door.]], you'll actually need to add a number, otherwise you'll always be opening the same door. This isn't dramatic, it's just numbering. It's not always enjoyable, so it'll be up to you to find various different formulas. When all is said and done, Twine offers you a nice way to write.

Twine doesn't handle conditionals either. A conditional? For example, if the character can open the door if he has the key, you have to write to paths: one where he has it and the other where he doesn't. You can't give him the key once reaches a certain point and put it in his inventory.

So, with Twine, the more conditionals, the more you reproduce, the more in the laborious part of the work. In sum, one could say it's a good school and that it teaches you to be in control of your story: you'll quickly avoid useless developments.

You could simply write some interactive text in Word and move about the document as you like, for example. With Twine, though, you can clearly see your arborescence. You see the branches to be developed and the branches in progress, and you can test out your story on a web browser, which is very practical.

So, want to give it a try?

For professionals

The advantage of Twine is that it's a free software you, your students, your interns, and your clients can easily install. Some can learn with it, others can see your mock-up.

Indeed, a text file with hypertext tags isn't always enough to show the interactivity to the client or the rest of your team. For this, Twine is very practical for quickly showing a rough sketch of the project.

We're very much talking about a rough sketch, here, because doing everything on Twine would be unproductive. You'd spend a crazy amount of time on it, and you'd have to start all over when start production. On the other hand, making a small story in broad strokes will be useful. You can present it all in a Twine file (tws) or even an HTML file that your client can send to collaborators without even having to install the software.

It's often difficult to come to an agreement on the vision of the project. With Twine, it's possible to make a small mock-up to quickly adjust course at the start: "Basically, isn't that what you want?" And afterward, all you have to do is discuss it.

We might as well let you know right away that, to insert an imported image, you need to put [IMG[relevantlink]] in the relevant block. And you have a small illustrated HTML file with the choices.

And to sum it all up, this prevents you from going overboard on the work, since it's just a rough sketch, since you haven't even been paid yet or you're just working on the pre-project, and the future isn't certain.

That being said, you can try a more powerful engine.

CELESTORY CREATOR

Accessible for beginners, this is a tool designed for professionals that allows you to generate numerous interactive story models.

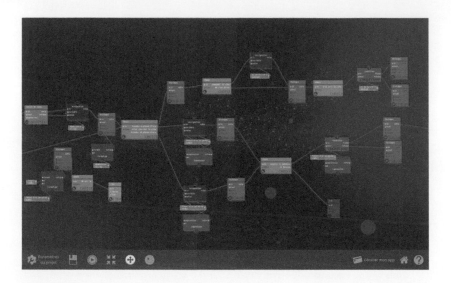

For beginners

With Celestory Creator, you can be guided at all stages when creating your interactive story. This contains everything from a methodology accompanied by graphic examples to your game design, whether a chat box, visual novel, interactive media or even an voice assistant app like Alexa.

You can even generate your own game application in order to start disseminating it and monetizing it in appstores without ever coding (even though there are some very advanced customization options for experts).

This is a very powerful tool. It lets you have fun developing your creativity with preexisting resources (such as visual packs of a universe) or customize the staging by directly importing yours.

You can also test out your stories in a preview mode that not only lets you visualize the variables of a part in real time but also change the UI (user interface) of the game and see how it changes.

For professionals

The advantage of being completely autonomous in the creation, the production, the testing and the distribution of your interactive story application is that you can then sell it around the world, whether directly to a client or to the general public in appstores.

Building a very customized simulation while also having a great ability to monitor an infinite number of variable changes is the real power of creating the data and getting to know your audience better.

Indeed, Celestory Creator uses variables (boolean, digital, text) that allow you to introduce conditionals.

Our character does or doesn't have the key to the door, or he needs the right number of keys, etc. In this way, you can refine your story and introduce a large number of elements. A health bar, for instance, is one of the most basic variables used.

So, while you'll have to use a bit of logic, not having to code is a relief, and if you need to get familiarized with the tool, you'll quickly make good use of the time you put into it.

Thus, with complete autonomy, you can fully write and create your video game with Celestory Creator and then monetize it.

PRO INSIGHT

Jean-Luc, what interactivity software do you use? How is the writing organized in a big production for a narrative-based game such a Life Is Strange? How does that all fit?

Jean-Luc Cano: I don't personally use any software. I write the arc, around 100 to 150 pages that tells the bulk of the story. Once that's done, we start producing the first episode by making the list of characters, the scenery, etc. Very often, there's too much. We put it all in the production grinder. We generally fuse places and characters to reduce things as much as possible. We always go from a general overview into the particulars. We start from an outline and go scene by scene.

David what tools do you use at Telltale to get ready for production?

With our experience, we knew how much time we would need with the right staff to create each scene depending on the length, the number of words written and the number spoken... We had all of these metrics we had recorded over the years. Thus, we used all these parameters. When we would create a new game, a new episode, we could predict how much time it would take us to build this game with the people we had. And when the script had been given to us, we had a thing called "the tool," which is preparatory software at Telltale. The authors had written their lines of dialogue in it and the production cost had been set. Each character had a specific cost center depending on its complexity and the number of assets needed to create it. This allowed us to optimize things, for example, to make already created characters say certain lines of dialogue to optimize the costs. The story was, then, linked to a production database.

OTHER TOOLS

There are several interactive scriptwriting tools, and each one has its advantages and disadvantages. Don't hesitate to try them out to see which one fits your interactive story best.

In particular, we can cite: Adrift, Inform, Conducttr, Chat Mapper and Inkle for text-based adventures, Visionaire Studio for point and click games, Tyrano Builder, VN Maker and Ren'Py for visual novels and Articy Draft for integrating with the Unity engine.

15. IMAGINING DIFFERENT ENDINGS

You've undoubtedly already read it in this book, the endings of an interactive story have a much greater impact on the a character than in an "ordinary" story. It's not at all about finding an ending, and if possible a good ending, but rather *many* endings, all of which have a benefit.

This is the power of interactivity: allowing the player to control her fate, or at least that of her heroine.

ALL ROADS DO NOT LEAD TO ROME

You can, even if it's not our focus here, make your paths all lead to the same ending, but in this case, you're drastically limiting the interactivity and the player's influence on the game, the player's journey. True, she'll be able to get to this ending with such a score, such clues unlocked, etc. but it will be the same ending in any case.

There's nothing keeping you from doing it, per se. This is often the case with choose-your-own-adventure books – when they first appeared, few offered very different endings, since the objective was to find the right way there. The limit on the number of paragraphs is a strong constraint, but it doesn't prevent you from offering different possible endings, however.

And to come to all these endings, since we're assuming you want to offer several of them, the player will not choose all the paths. True, you can make it so at the end of your story the heroine has a crucial choice to make that will lead her to such or such ending, but, okay, that's a little easy, isn't it? However, this also depends on your game specifications, your objective and your lead time.

The notion of lead time is important: the more endings you offer, the longer you'll need to write the interactive story you've imagined. It's incompressible.

INTERACTIVE SCRIPTWRITING, RETRO-WRITING?

Why is it necessary to know the endings? This will help you better manage planning for your writing, by knowing how long you'll need. And this will allow you to think about the construction of the story. You'll need to write in a backward direction.

It's possible to compare interactive writing with writing crime novels, the kind with mysteries, the famous whodunits or game novels. The goal of this type of book is to allow the reader guess, or at least try to guess, who's the culprit at the end. And to guide and confuse the reader, the writer must have an idea of the motive, the culprit, the means, the place, in sum everything concerning the crime and how the detective is going to solve the mystery. Then he's going to sprinkle clues and red herrings throughout the story. This doesn't mean he writes his chapters in a backward direction, but when he writes the text from A to Z, he'll know where to place a clue or throw the reader off.

As you can see, it's well and truly a game. If you imagine different endings, this will help you considerably in creating your arborescence and the forks where the paths taken by the player won't intersect again.

If your heroine must become spiderwoman (or not), there will be a sudden fork, the scene where she gets bitten by the spider (or not). In an interactive narrative, she can very well squash the spider without stopping the story at all. And if there's a transformation, you're right to guess that as she becomes spiderwoman, the player will have the possibility to be more than just a superheroine. With an easy pun, we can see the web of the story being woven.

In the event your heroine becomes spiderwoman, you can obviously see the other two big possible endings, supervillain or superheroine. But she may also use her powers for her own purposes, which may not necessarily be tyranny, but rather an industrial empire specializing in hight quality apparel made from her webbing. And here, her competitors want to discover her secret, and now you're off again...

It's easy to let your imagination run wild, and necessary, but mustn't start writing right away.

MAIN ENDINGS AND SECONDARY ENDINGS

You're writing interaction. There will be endings that players will choose massively and others a lot less. And it's in great part because of you.

You're offering an interactive story, or stories, but there will truly be some royal votes. In our example of spiderwoman, we feel the choice of the superheroine or supervillain is not only an obvious proposition but also a necessary one in superhero universes.

Moreover, there are other main endings, for example where the heroine uses her power solely for her own enrichment, without the desire for tyranny, or where she avoids the spider bite and finds herself recruited by an army of extra-terrestrials. These endings are less obvious than the previous ones. Culturally, less players will choose them, but you must never neglect their curiosity and their desire to approach a genre in a totally different way.

In total, here we have four big endings, four main endings. But the reality is that in a game, there is a strong likelihood that, statistically, the two special endings will be played less and become secondary. If you want to keep them as main endings, in the arborescence, you'll have to insist and make it so that the player can seriously reflect on this type of choice.

Even for you, in creating your story, there will be endings you like more than others, and you'll have a tendency to insist on these paths, to offer more interactions, to fuss over them, etc. Be careful, even if you dreamed of playing a mega-rich heroine who made her fortune with ultra-resistant clothing made with a revolutionary fiber, your story must allow each player to have fun with each proposed path. Unless you deliberately leave clues along the way to offer punitive paths that the player will knowingly choose, you mustn't neglect the paths to the main endings.

Does this mean you should disregard the secondary endings? First, we need to make sure we're on the same page with this term. For us, this means any kinds of endings that shorten the game: the death of the heroine, her fleeing, her rejection of the adventure, etc.

If your player is going against the game, because she's in a bad mood or wants see what absurdity her absurd choices lead to, you're not going to waste your time writing an uninteresting branch that leads nowhere.

On the other hand, by guiding her to choices that make her really hesitate, you can lead her to make a bad choice, i.e. a choice leading her to a secondary ending, and offer her an interesting, though fatally shorter, ending to her adventure. You superheroine prefers to retire and live in the jungle with spiders. It's probably not worth it to have her live in the jungle, the story stops once she gets there. And of course don't hesitate to add a mushroom cloud when the big villain obliterates the city.

Naturally, the story could continue in the jungle. She discovers a uranium mine and an arachnid civilization, etc. Here's there reason why you need to know from the start where you're leading the player, and whether an ending will be a main one or secondary one. Our arachnid civilization story is a main ending, so you take the time to write it. In your adventures, you player must sense, guess and know that there is something play there. If it's just a simple proposition to go on vacation in the Yucatan, it might be overlooked. And your main ending turns into a secondary ending, even very secondary, even though you put a crazy amount of time into it.

This is very clear: the secondary endings can be endings that you would have loved to have developed more – which you chose to not do from the beginning. And since they are secondary endings, you mustn't dedicate a large part of your story to them.

REPLAYABILITY AND CHARACTERIZATION OF ENDINGS

The more you make the player feel that she had crucial choices and other possibilities, the more you increase the appeal to replay the game. But bear in mind that, initially, replaying a game is first and foremost starting over because you failed along the way.

So, you need to dedicate yourself the experience the player is going to live more so than the notion of replayability. The player may very well content herself to play a game with multiple endings, but one that will have challenged her and offered her the opportunity to live something intense. It's her choice to replay the game or not. You can make it so that your player lives a great moment, but clearly have less of an ability to make her play the game over in its entirety, even if there are clearly other paths.

The player is the one who decides how many times she's going to play the game. The better it is, the more she'll play it and the more she'll feel like replaying it, or she'll recommend it to others. Many games simply offer varying degrees of difficulty, and that is enough to ensure replayability.

Don't worry, you will inevitably think about replayability when you think about the different endings. By characterizing your endings, you will naturally create replayability. If we take our example of the superheroine, players will certainly try the game in at least two ways, the path of good and the path of evil.

FROM MANICHEISM TO PLURALITY

To conclude this chapter, it's important to recognize that offering an ending where the main character is good, or even bad, is as appealing as it is expected. You'll undoubtedly offer these two main endings. For one very simple reason: the other paths are often more vague, more subtle, and won't be as drastically different from each other. When you play an extreme character, a fanatic of good or an evil crusader, the absence of compromise inevitably pits these two types of ending against each other.

Everything depends on your project, but you already know that working the other endings will always be more delicate. We recommend that you, first, think of the extremes, which will also define your scope of reflection, and to then see to what extent another path is possible in these stories. It will be very beneficial to know how to divert a character initially committed to such or such path to another that isn't diametrically opposed. These have a high likelihood of being secondary endings, but working on them as main endings will be the little extra something that gives your interactive story flavor.

Defining the endings allows you to direct the choices, the trigger events redirect them

TIs, rather TEs (trigger events), allow you to control the story. Here, Ending 1 takes priority.

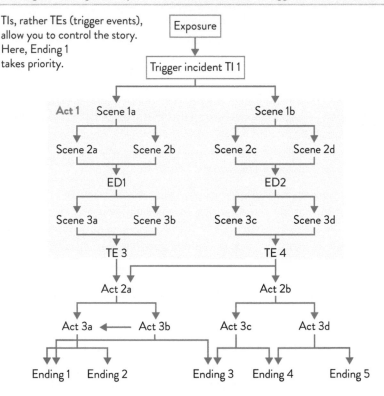

PRO INSIGHT

David, how do you manage your different endings in an interactive story?

David Cage: I don't like linear stories that offer five different endings. For me, they are not interactive stories, but rather interactive endings. The interactivity has to be present in each scene and not just in the ending. In *Detroit*, from the very first scene we made an attempt to think of the different ways each scene can be played, the consequences of each decision and the impact they will have on the story. Everything becomes interactive and ramified. The tree of possible narratives naturally grows until it virtually explodes at the end of the story.

The last act in *Detroit* is full of ramifications because we had to deal with all the consequences of all the preceding scenes.

Sybil, how do you plan the different endings of an interactive story?

Sybil Collas: The endings need to reflect two things, the player's choices and the character's evolution. To build different endings with an equivalent emotional charge, there needs to be a contrast among them, and they need to underscore how the story has made both the character and the player evolve. It's important to identify a set of strong, familiar markers: from the beginning up to the ending, what important, identifiable aspects of the character, the gameplay and the world, have changed? Is the way of playing the relationship of trust between the characters, like between Kratos and Atreus, or Naia and Naiee? Is the player's thirst for blood like in *Undertale*, *The Wolf Among Us*, or *Vampyr*?

These markers are valuable and dictate what the player needs to pay attention to. Since most players don't finish a video game they've started (According to Microsoft Studio, in 2014), identifying the "endings" becomes less important than identifying the "changes." These evolution markers need to be identifiable throughout the story, and not just in its endings. They are a benefit to the player and highlight the DNA of the topic of your story. The ending should be nothing other than the logical conclusion of the game's progression and a final reward to the story defined by the player's actions.

Joe, how do you think about the endings in an interactive narrative?

Joe Pinney: Creating several satisfying endings in a story is a difficult task. You mustn't just add endings for the joy of offering more and more choices. Each ending needs to make sense. You have to illustrate the fundamental dilemma the player is facing. In *Wolf Among Us*, it's about protecting the people you love. Is it better to be brutal, and risk being hated, or nice, and risk being ineffective? There's no good answer, it's up to the player to decide. Whatever path the player takes, honor this choice, play the consequences, whether good or bad.

FibreTigre, how do you conceive your endings in an interactive narrative?

FibreTigre: The ending is what's most important. I don't start writing until I have a noteworthy ending that rewards the player, that really brings the story to a close, a modern ending that stands on its own and makes sense. If the budget allows, you can make several noteworthy endings, but the real difficulty is not privileging one over another and leading people to believe there is only one orthodox ending.

For the occasional deaths during the game, they need to be short but memorable.

16. THE DIFFERENT TYPES OF CHOICES

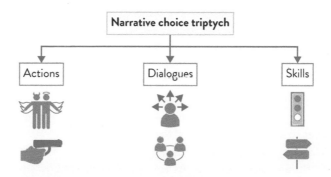

There are different types of choices:

- Action choices highlight your player's moral point of view. *I act, therefore I assume the consequences.* These choices allow you to draw up a profile of your player. Indeed, above all, the decisions we make say something about who we are.

- Dialogue choices allow you to personalize your main character. Each secondary character will have a particular point of view based on your attitude, both in public and in private.

- Skill choices In an action game, if the player develops skills with firearms or, the opposite, skills in discretion, she will undoubtedly attack the enemy base in the first case, while in the second case, she'll certainly choose to infiltrate it.

Note: All of these choices have consequences on the evolution of the environment. Here, we're talking about the background characters or the game universe itself. You character is connected to the world around him, and the consequences must be felt in the farthest reaches of the world you've built.

Choice is an essential element of an interactive story. So, if you're in a story that is more action based, you need to make choices fast to survive and continue the adventure.

This chapter on choices is essentially concerned with stories where the player sees the choices that are offered to her. We're in interactive storytelling. If your project is about eliminating Nazis with a machine gun 60% of the time, you don't need to read these lines.

PRO INSIGHT

David, how does the player perceive the consequences of his choices? With what kind of feedback?

David Cage: When you work on interactive storytelling, one of the challenges is offering the player choices he can perceive the consequences of.

We've tried many different things over the years. I've always loved organic storytelling because I always thought the player didn't have a need to know all the secrets of the narrative or the writing.

With *Beyond: Two Souls*, however, I realized that, when the choices aren't very clear, the player has a tendency to think the narrative is linear. In *Heavy Rain*, for example, we had a car chase scene where the player had to hit the buttons the right way at the right time to keep the car he was chasing in sight. The players who didn't managed to keep pace with the car thought that it was the only way to finish the scene, however you could actually continue the chase for a while and catch up to your target at the end.

With *Detroit*, we did things a bit differently to make sure the player would see and understand the choices while also realizing that he could have chosen something completely different.

We also decided to portray the arborescence of possible choices at the end of each scene. At the start, I was really resisted the idea of implementing this feature, but we realized this choice was incredibly popular with the players because most of them assessed how they played a scene and thought they had made the best possible choices. And, then, they see the arborescence and realize all of the ramifications they didn't explore, which makes them want to replay each scene to see each branch.

For me, one of the secrets of offering the player interesting choices is to make sure the player is conscious of the moments where he makes choices and how serious these decisions are.

Joe, how do you organize the choices in an interactive story?

Joe Pinney: I start with the story arc I want the player to face as a whole and the choices that involves. For example, let's say it's a story about an idealist facing a harsh reality. Perhaps at a given time, the idealist will have to choose between his ideals and the happiness of someone dear to him. I think about how to make these choices interesting and difficult. Quickly, I have some choices and major events on a time line. I break it down into scenes, I determine what each scene is about and what other choices could go with it. Over time, I give the choices for each dialogue more depth. Each choice has to matter one way or another, or appear to matter, or otherwise, the player won't care. Ideally, each choice increases the player's sense of commitment to the story and the characters, and leads to a powerful ending.

FibreTigre, how do you organize the choices in an interactive narrative?

FibreTigre: All the choices need to make sense, be probable and credible, and must follow a set of long, basic rules as described by Graham Nelson, for example: you must get fair warning when one of your choices will arbitrarily lead to death. Making sense is essential: you can have a game doesn't save, for example. It's a terrible idea, but if the nature of the game justifies it, it's accepted.

Thomas, how do you organize the choices in an interactive narrative?

Thomas Veauclin: The main idea is not have cosmetic choices. We have some, but very few. Once we established this vision, for *The Council* we decided there would be no manual saving in the game. The game automatically saves on a regular basis. So, you can't go back by going to where you last saved. All this led us to establish one last rule: there are no bad choices.

A player's choice is inevitably a good choice because it's his. So, we must respect it and assume it. Whether these choices are moral or not doesn't change a thing. In reality, everything is a choice in a video game. Beginning with the door to the right and the one to the left, it's a choice. Choosing a response in a dialogue is obviously a choice, but develop such or such *skill* is one too. Doing only what is asked of you or searching everywhere are also choices. Whatever the player does, he decides.

THE ILLUSION OF CHOICE?

Let us first lay this cornerstone of the interactive story. Your objective is to make the player live an adventure. and involve her by making her own choices lead to a fate that gradually reveals itself. Thus, you need to maintain suspense.

However, it will be difficult for you to continually offer crucial choices, unsustainable dilemmas. The longer the player's experience is, the more complicated it will be.

You can always make an illusion of it, in the positive sense of the term. Don't forget that the player never knows all the consequences of a choice. You're the one who decides that. Obviously, if this is totally unrelated, your adventure will be over quickly.

With the illusion of choice, we propose all these choices the consequences of which are, ultimately, insignificant; however, if the player happens to have doubts, she cannot be certain.

PRO INSIGHT

David, certain choices are very intense and really turn a story upside down while others are less important. What do you think of the idea of "the illusion of choice?"

David Cage: In *Detroit*, there really is the illusion of choice. We decided not to offer choices that wouldn't influence the story. To do this, we had to accept the fact that we were going to create content that would only be played by 10% of the players. Ultimately, it's not a problem, since these players will talk about their experience and will make other players want to explore this branch that they may not have see the first time they played the game.

Concerning choices, there are obviously several categories. It is impossible to only have choices that will completely change the story. It's not feasible. We have some choices that will have consequences in the scene, others that will have consequences in the next scene and, lastly, the most important choices that will have a significant impact on the whole story.

We offer the player the chance to make decisions that completely change the narrative and lead him to branches that he never who have been able to explore otherwise. In *Detroit*, it was one of our main challenges: write the content, test it, film it and implement it knowing that this content will only be played by a small fraction of the players. But that is an integral part of the concept and the artistic choices we made.

Thomas, how does one give the illusion that anything is possible?

Thomas Veauclin: You need two fundamental elements. First, the player's trust. Begin by offering him some choices with immediate, very different consequences in order to establish a relationship of trust with him. He needs to play your game, not defy you. If you're making this game, it's for him, so give it to him. You mustn't ever deceive him. When you know that a situation must involve a certain consequence, assume it. If you cannot assume it, don't create this situation.

Secondly, get his attention. Don't so far as sleight of hand, but that's sort of the idea. Place a player in the desert. For a long time. For a very long time. What's he going to think of the second he gets out? Drinking water. You can create ten different paths, 98% of users will choose drinking water.

I'm not a soothsayer. I created his desire, his need. This is the very principle of advertising and marketing. There have been a good number of experiments on this subject in order to understand the human reactions. We are easily influenced. Naturally. So, you can steer the choices. But there is one rule you must never break: never deceive the player!

In the dialogues

You can particularly use this for a dialogue during exchanges between the main character and another. There are several benefits to this:

- You set the tone of the dialogue, an atmosphere.
- Your player learns how to interact with this character.
- You can place some clues.

The point of your conversations mustn't be to fill out your story, far from it, but all these little choices allow the player to play her role, and to choose the tone of the relationships she wants to have with such or such character. And, yes, these choices can, over the course of the conversation, have an impact on the clues that the character reveals to her, or influence the future behavior of this character.

Put one after another, these choices matter, but individually, they are not crucial for the story. Return to the chapter about dialogues, but these choices are based on the way in which the dialogues serve the story.

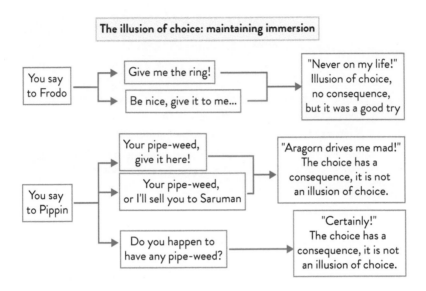

The illusion of choice: maintaining immersion

You say to Frodo → Give me the ring! / Be nice, give it to me... → "Never on my life!" Illusion of choice, no consequence, but it was a good try

You say to Pippin → Your pipe-weed, give it here! / Your pipe-weed, or I'll sell you to Saruman → "Aragorn drives me mad!" The choice has a consequence, it is not an illusion of choice.

Do you happen to have any pipe-weed? → "Certainly!" The choice has a consequence, it is not an illusion of choice.

In the action

Choices don't just concern the dialogues, obviously there are the main character's actions. Perhaps even more than compared to a character, the player has trouble assessing the consequences of her choices. Opening a door is always perilous in a game.

So, you can offer the player different choices to open it, but you, in sum, in your story, you know this door reveals this or that if it gets opened regardless of the choice selected to open it. Thus, there is an illusion of choice, insofar as you can do whatever you want to open the door, the result will be the same. The real choice will be whether to open the door or not.

This basic example illustrates that in action, you can multiply the methods of resolving an action, but these methods don't have an impact on the story or the path taken by the player. On the other hand, this is unadulterated gaming, the player enjoys choosing and applying a method.

And from time to time, you'll have taken care to place a crucial choice there. As such, your player will never know whether she's making an insignificant choice or, conversely, whether she's worrying about something important.

Remember that the brain reactions very good to conditioning. If an action resolved with such a choices gives the same result n times, you'll easily trap her when, on the $n+1$ time, you opt for a different resolution for the same choice. It's up to you to provide the player with elements that warn her of the change ahead of time, or not.

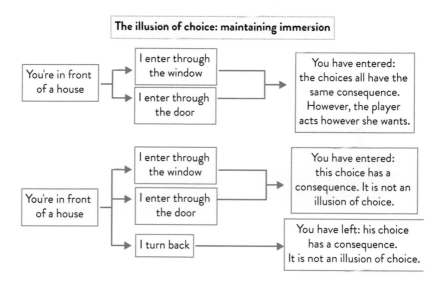

The illusion of choice: maintaining immersion

CRUCIAL CHOICES

Or the art of the dilemma. Your player understands she is faced with a choices the consequences of which will weigh on the rest of the adventure. True, you can cause her false fear or false joy, but it's best not to abuse this. If your choices too often have unexpected circumstances, unless you're in a universe designed for that (burlesque, strange, etc.), your player will end up choosing at random, and it's quite likely she'll become uninterested with the adventure.

Benjamin, what are the advantages and inconveniences of interactive directing?

Benjamin Diebling: Often, a perverse thing happens writing an interactive story: you have a tendency to prefer one choice over another. As a scriptwriter, you need to beware of that. Each choice needs to be interesting because the risk is that all the people who interact with your interactive story will make the same choice. You mustn't condemn a branch to a default choice. What you need to do when you direct a scene is to have a dialogue, a way of filming, music, an environment that makes each choice important, beautiful, interesting, intriguing. That's the most important. You need to give players interesting choices in writing, but also visually, so that they get the impression that, whatever choice they are faced with, interesting things will happen.

What ways are there to make the player understand that his choice will matter?

There are consequences, either right away or later. They can be visual, auditory or related to the narrative. For example, when the player chooses to shoot: he shoots, that's visual. That's right away. The music following the choices can get more somber or lighter: it's an immediate auditory consequence. You can also have choices that have delayed consequences on the narrative. For example, if the player has chosen to beat someone, a few choices later, a character refuses to help him because the beaten person was that person's mother... The best thing is to make a mix of the immediate or almost immediate consequences and the delayed consequences, and not content yourself with doing just one type of consequence.

How do we divide up the short, medium and long term consequences?

You need to test things out, by reflecting on the writing, by imagining; you film the consequences by adding ideas that could influence the choices.

In the dialogues

This time, the context, the situation makes it so the player cannot be mistaken; you know the character or characters facing you is/are going to react to what your main character is going to say. Incomprehension being a bane of humanity, in this situation your player will more easily accept unexpected reactions relating to her own choices, particularly if there is a big cultural difference (a cowboy vis-à-vis an Indian, an explorer vis-à-vis an Alpha-Centaurian, etc.).

Nevertheless, this choice is going to trigger a reaction that is going to shift the attitude of the secondary character. This choice may have been prepared by a multitude of insignificant choices over the course of the dialogue that have steered the conversation in this direction, and now's the time everything will be decided.

Never forget that the player forgets. Put another way, when a choice has consequences, she needs to see it so she'll remember it later. Otherwise, as your story continues, the secondary character's behavior may seem incoherent to her.

In the action

Very often, choices will have physical consequences for the main character, or for a secondary character. The matter of life or death is one the most frequent crucial choices. But saving some equipment, finding an item, decoding something, etc. can also a crucial choice: the player just needs to be aware of it, or at least think about it.

Indeed, it's too easy to leave an item lying around, and if the player has the good sense to grab it, it'll save her skin later on. Such an item shouldn't just be picked up at random. We should be encouraged to pick it up, or something should make us hesitate to pick it up.

What we want to get across is that if frustration is a means of motivating the player, making her lose just because she didn't open the right door without having any idea of how or why is counterproductive.

Along the same line of thought, if time is against the player, she needs to find out or guess sooner or later because her choices in the action will be connected. She will know that she's taking a risk on choices that waste time, even if it's perhaps the only valid option to solve a problem.

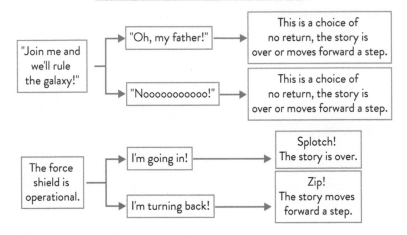

STEERING CHOICES

Your player makes choices depending on what her character lives, and depending on what she chooses for him. Thus, if she wants an aggressive character, she will generally choose to be aggressive both in the dialogues and in the action, and, in return, she will be offered choices linked to her own behavior.

Guiding the player

At the start of the game, it's not a bad idea to offer a series of questions to take control of the game, regardless of the media you're preparing your interactive story for. In the part about introductions, think of how to make intro fun, interactive and educational. The more you can prevent the player from having to read pages of rules or do a tutorial, the faster she'll be able to start the adventure. But this depends on you project.

In any case, you can then, in the way you write the possible choices, guide your player towards the right solution. "Are you certain you want to call the quarter master?" At first, when reading this, we may not be sure, especially without context. If, beforehand, the player heard strange sounds on the deck and a trail of blood is leading out from under the cabin door, perhaps it's not a good idea. If, on the other hand, someone were to say there is a party on the deck, this seems less risky.

And the choices aren't necessarily written: in your story you can provide visual choices, audio, etc. You need to pay attention to the context, but if you've locked your main character in a closed down morgue, would it better for him to go to where he hears shuffling or in the opposite direction? He only has choices of direction to make, but the soundscape may serve as a guide. If your player knows that she's in a zombie universe, she will undoubtedly avoid shuffling noises...

When you write a choice to guide the player, always pay attention to the context in which she's going to make her decision. Which brings us to another possibility.

Misleading the player

You also have the possibility of leading the player to her perdition, or to a more enviable punishment. As we have already mentioned, language is your work tool.

Consequently, you can create tension, and a false indication with "Are you sure?", "Do you want to take the risk?", etc. True, this isn't exactly misleading the player unless you've previously conditioned her to make a positive choice when she sees these kinds of phrases.

The order of the choices offered in writing is never innocuous. The first choice is always overvalued by the player. And the shortest choices among longer ones can be disregarded.

If you trick your player, try to give her a clue beforehand to warn her – perhaps she won't choose the right path, too bad for her character.

You're the scriptwriter, so you can do anything you want, and if you don't give the player any chance, she'll no longer be actively playing, she'll be having things happen to her, which is the opposite of interactive gameplay.

REFOCUSING ATTENTION

You're making an interactive story. Whatever media you're writing for, do not turn you player into a spectator. You can do it for specific sequences that serve the plot or the atmosphere of the story, and if possible both, but don't repeat this kind of thing too often. Your player mustn't be just a player who hits the buttons enough to start the next sequence.

In an interactive story, you interact. Hence, the aforementioned importance of the illusion of choice: it's better to offer a small series of insignificant choices, at least individually but eventually forming a group, than to space out the player's decisions too often.

PLACING THE CHOICES BASED ON THE MEDIA

The choices you offer will appear differently depending on how offer your adventure for such or such media.

For roleplaying games

The choices for an action are often offered in terms of a test. For dialogues, as stated in the relevant chapter, it's better to provide lots of lines. In a roleplaying game, the gamemaster is the person who proposes the choices for the players to make, and the players will undoubtedly have other ideas too. Concretely, more than anything the gamemaster proposes a situation (a fortress to infiltrate, a person to interrogate), and the players will decide themselves why and how to act. The role you will play will consist of suggesting solutions to the problem (a certain password allows you to enter the fortress, speaking about the witness's childhood makes him crack). You provide some keys, but you can't offer all the choices.

For a choose-your-own-adventure book

You are in the media with the most writing, and in which the gameplay is inevitably tied to the reading. At the end of a paragraph, you'll either have a list of choices or phrases ending in "go to n," etc. The choices at the end of the paragraphs in the form of phrases are the most immersive. This interrupts the player's reading the least. A simple list is sometimes necessary, but it will remove the player from the atmosphere – even though she very well knows she's playing the book and not reading it. You can also slip choices into an illustration.

For a comic book

Space is tight and expressing choices with text is easy, but you have to be concise. However, it often seems logical to offer some in the illustrations themselves; it's important to use the graphic power of this medium as much as possible. Given that it's graphic in nature, you need to think of your choices this way too. For a visual novel, let's say a digital comic book, you can make the choices similar to those in video games, but always bear in mind that your players like the graphic aspect of your game. That's its power.

For radio

The difficulty of pure audio is that it demands a lot of the player's ability to pay attention. So, if you provide a lot of choices, take care not to lose her. And you either provide very short sequences between each decision, or you cram all of the elements needed to make a decision at the end of the sequence, i.e. scene. An inattentive player may choose at random. If the listening time is long, you need to make sure you accustom the player so that she knows she needs to pay attention before it's time for the choices.

For audiovisual

There are different ways to come to the choices. In this media, the illusion of choices is perhaps to be preferred more than in any other. Indeed, if you have already read a good part of this book, you know that filming is complicated to do and costly. So, stringing together some inconsequential choices that lead the player to the same scene regardless of here choices allow you to refocus attention before offering choices that will generate different results.

For a video game

As with audiovisual, the ways of offering choices vary greatly, but you are don't have the hard constraint of filming. So, it's here where you need to be careful. You have more freedom, so always think about the pacing and the atmosphere you're giving to your story. It's no good making your main character choose in a calm setting all the time as in an Agatha Christie investigation, but you might have some "bourgeois" choices to maintain the atmosphere (What fork for the fish?). Whereas in a survival style game like *Predator*, your heroine is often going to have to choose quickly, and the consequences can be serious. First, determine the pacing and the style, always take a look at the technical constraints, and spread out your choices.

Jean-Luc, isn't it difficult to create characters knowing they can change in the interactive narrative depending on the player's actions?

Jean-Luc Cano: No, because it's an illusion. The author always controls everything in the background. He's the one who chooses how the character changes after the player's action. The author writes the choices and the paths. So, when I write, I control the changes on all the possibilities.

This must require you to foresee quite a lot of possibilities?

No, because with interactive gaming, you make the illusion there are consequences. The choices involve different scenes and various paths, but there are mandatory scenes that the player is inevitably going to go through, in order to rationalize the branches and group together the possibilities. There are core elements common to all the choices. The consequences can arrive in the short, medium or long term, or not at all.

You only put short, medium or long-term consequences?

Before determining the consequences, it's necessary to write a general arc. First, I write the big parts of the story, then episode by episode, I go more in depth into the story and I write the short, medium and long-term consequences.

Would you say there are different types of choices? Could you classify them?

Indeed, there are different types of choices. In terms of hierarchy, first there is survival: choices of life or death. Then, there are moral choices. Lastly, there are day-to-day choices, such as picking up the telephone, for example. These little choices often seem insignificant, but they can have can have very big consequences over the course of the story. Is it up to the player to be shrewd and create the consequences he wants.

Aren't you afraid of losing the player if he isn't informed of the consequences of his choices?

No, because in the end, it's like it is in real life. We can never really know the consequences of our acts, even if sometimes we doubt them. So, it's not necessary to reveal them in a video game.

So, you don't prepare the players to make fully informed decisions?

No, I do not give them advance warning. If you know the consequences, you choose your choices. It's not necessary to steer the players, so that they can make their choices with their sensibility, and so that, in this way, they can discover themselves. Everything we do in life has consequences, if one of choices has a bad consequence, it's not a big deal, that's life. It's the same in the game.

17. THE GRAPH BESTIARY

Now that you're beginning to get a better idea of interactive scriptwriting, here are some conceptual graphs that may give you an idea. These are meant to be taken figuratively. They help work your imagination, an imagination based on technique and practice.

Don't hesitate to name your graphs and give them a purpose, or even symbolism!

THE SNAIL

In this graph, the player can explore at her leisure, until an element programmed or triggered by her moves the story forward.

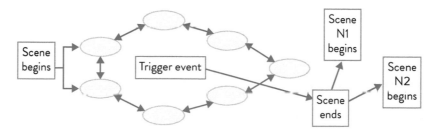

THE DUCK FOOT

This graph corresponds to the moment where the player makes choices that steer the adventure. It is possible for her to navigate before making a choice crucial to the ending. Beware of a combinatorial explosion.

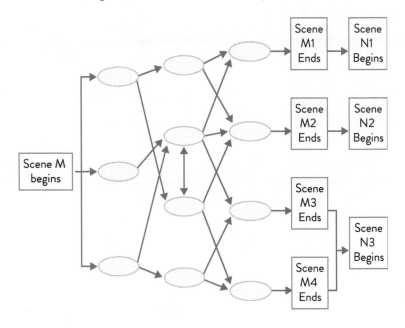

THE OCTOPUS

This graph corresponds to the moment where the player makes a crucial choice that steers her adventure right away, and from here there's no way back.

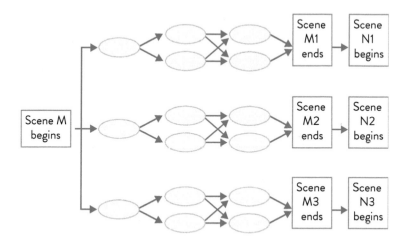

THE ANT-LION

In this graph, the player will have plenty to think about. She'll take the desired path. This is ideal for narrowing the plot without wanting to deliberately create an event.

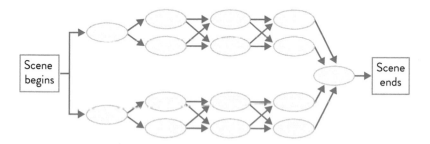

THE CENTIPEDE

This graph is ideal for a chase, a test, or an action where it's better to not make mistakes.

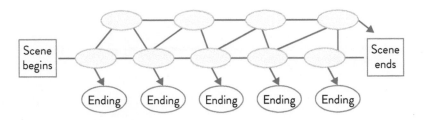

THE BLOWFISH

This graph is ideal for a conversation among characters. The center is blown up by illusions of choice. Only the later choices matter.

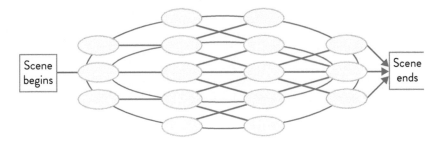

18. THE POWER OF CONSTRAINTS

This chapter is going to concern you, as well as the player or the main character: we will address the specific constraints for each.

FOR THE CHARACTERS

The main character

This has already been addressed in the chapters on the characters: your main character must be motivated. And constraints are good motivators. Anything that threatens the health, good fortune, family, etc. of your main character is a constraint.

We use is so often, that sometimes we end up not even thinking about it anymore, but time is a common constraint. Any human activity is constrained by time. It seems natural that time would a constraint for the main character. For MMORPGs we can tell you that time is no longer a constraint for the character, but it definitely still is for the player.

Your main character can also motivated by something other than a constraint (for example, altruism, love, etc.), but it's necessary to recognize that, even if he's not forced by something, it is his moral code, his attitude that is going to push him to act, imposing a form of constraint. Be it as it may, the main character must be warned of the constraints weighing on him, or those he'll want to take well into consideration. If a stop-watch is started, it's necessary for him to have the chance to know there is a countdown, to suspect something.

These constraints weighing on the main character are going to have an impact on his means of action. And sometimes he'll be willing to do anything to succeed, annihilating even the codes of morality; other times, he'll have to walk on eggshells if a punishment threatens to befall him or those close to him.

A constraint allows you to stop the main character if, by certain behaviors, he threatens to destroy your entire story. On the other hand, this can push him to act in the main directions. Attention: if you make a story that steers too much, this may bore the player.

Secondary characters

Let's not forget them, but their own motivations are often galvanized or restrained by their own constraints. They have a tyrannical master or are compulsive killers, but in building your story, your secondary characters may, if a listening situation, express to the main character the constraints weighing on them. These constraints can be used as leverage for him to help them or use them as part of his own mission, his own adventure.

If you're in an interactive narrative, the interaction with the secondary characters should allow them to express their constraints, or conversely, if we dare say, their motivations. It is important that the main character, and thus the player, understand his universe and the story. And constraints are a good means of forcing a secondary character to reveal his role. Whether by force, persuasion, observation, seduction, conviction, etc., your main character must have the chance to figure out the set of cogs and pulleys that make your secondary characters tick.

FOR THE PLAYER

For the player, constraints represent the challenges one must overcome. They're what give the game flavor. This isn't necessarily a series of fights you have to win in record time with a sole weapon, but developing an ecosystem in a terraforming project won't be a cakewalk either.

The main character's constraints are, by definition, the player's constraints. Thus, she must really take control of what happens to your main character, whether it's to play as the character, if you've specifically developed her role, or to leave her own imprint on him, for example with a character suffering from amnesia — even if this example is somewhat extreme.

Don't forget either that the player has her own constraints, not the least of which is the game time. This is obvious, but it serves to remind us that it's necessary for something to happen in our story. And in your project if there is not benefit to making the player experience a ten-month voyage to Mars in real time, then use ellipses. That aside, if you have a game project spanning years, it is as you feel it. Now that we're connected all the time, that changes many things.

The game time is something you must bear in mind; it shapes how you envision your interactive story. And the player must have an idea of the average time your story is going to take her. We know very well that an average time is not the actual time. From there, it's up to her to spend more time or not exploring other branches in your interactive story.

FOR THE AUTHOR

You are the first person concerned by constraints. The first out of all of them is certainly the time and the retroplanning to write your story.

One inevitably lacks enough time, this is the tragedy of the human condition. However, you can transform this constraint into a strength: this limited time can push you to do something.

In your case, the deadline is going to motivate you to write: no procrastinating. So, yes, some days, it will be better to keep your imagination in check — it's not because you're blanking, it's that your brain is thinking things over. Don't hesitate to change ideas, but stay focused: you have a text to write. At least try to sit down at your keyboard. You'll be surprised to see that, sometimes, things come all by themselves. Conversely, it's possible to run out of words quickly during a false start.

It's up to you to manage these constraints, and instead of hitting your head against a wall when things don't come to you, rejoice, it's an opportunity to do something else. After, it will go much better when you resume work. But you need to maintain this discipline: everyday you need to evaluate where you're at, and see if you're ahead of schedule or behind. Unfortunately, anytime you get ahead of schedule, you eventually lose it. That's just how it goes. On the other hand, when you get behind, since you regularly assess your progress, is the kick in the behind that's going to get you moving when the time comes.

Are you working on a personal project? Set a date, not least of all to see where you're at a given time (1% or 58%, for example). Some projects take years to see the light of day because writing is a long adventure.

We won't go on forever about this subject because there is another fundamental constraint: the budget. You can do anything when writing a story, but depending on the media and the project's budget, you'll more likely being doing a short film or saga, more likely doing a casual game than a visual novel, etc.

Find out about the project so you can make a suitable story. To do this, as we've stated several times in this book, dialogue with people, exchange information with them. Everyone has see, read and played stories, but writing them is different, and your colleagues, your boss, etc. often have a biased idea for the pure and simple reason that it's not their trade. If what they are telling you is not feasible, you need to tell them.

Next, if you're budget is limited, this is going to lead to find writing tricks to achieve your objectives. Did you want such or such scene but it won't be possible (too many illustrations, animations, etc.)? You'll find a way to bring it about, not the least of which is having it be told by other characters. Exchange information with the developers, the graphic designers, etc. If there's a part of the story that you envision but think might be hard to pull off, put your trust in them, they might have a very simple solution, or they'll find one for you.

Does it bear repeating that specifications can be a big constraint? You very well may have accepted a job to pay the bills, since in our societies we live to pay.

You're going to have to adapt to such a project, by gathering documentation, of course, but also by using this constraint to your advantage, looking at it as a challenge: how are you going to write a story about the Olympic Games even though you've never taken an interest in sports? If you focus on the negative, you will truly have a rough time. You need to address the problem as an opportunity to develop your skills, to show that you know how to write, even with a subject that's not really your cup of tea. And why? Not to so you can be a winner and smile smugly, but because if you tackle the subject head on, you'll finish it on time: there is nothing worse than taking an eternity to write a subject you're not passionate about, so it's better to get it done and over with.

REACHING POINTS OF NO RETURN

You're writing an interactive story that contains several stories. These stories move forward gradually as your player lives them. And this player makes choices, but for everything to remain coherent, certain choices, particularly crucial choices, need to be definitive: there's no turning back.

And it's not just about backing up. In interactive story writing, it is tempting to create multiple branches, jump from one to another, connect one to another, etc., but your story must move forward. For everything to remain coherent, when the player chooses certain branches of the story, she is steering herself toward a path that she may still be able to change in some way, but the choice is been made and is final.

Thus, there is something matter of fact about this. When the player opens one door, other doors close, and there is naturally some dramatic tension: putting points of no return makes the player understand that the adventure continues on. Even if you are in a story where the heroine can walk about freely, if you've written a story, at certain points, it is necessary to understand that things move forward, the story continues on, perhaps even without the player.

This is interactive storywriting: you can allow the player the chance to leave the story, but she real needs to understand what she's doing.

PRO INSIGHT

David, how do you place points of no return in your stories?
David Cage: I don't really think in terms of points of no return. The story is what dictates what is needed. The player makes choices from the very first scene, choices that will have an impact later on in the story. However, these aren't points of no return insofar as this impact can evolve in many ways.

Certain choices are cut and dry and are not consequences of your last ten hours playing. So, the player knows that if he decides this instead of that, it will be a definitive choice. It's the nature of the choices that requires this, and the player understands that certain choices are definitive, while others are not.

19. A PERSONALIZED EXPERIENCE

You player must live a unique experience. Like a person reading a book or watching a film, she may have read the same book or watched the same film as thousands of other people, but her experience will be unique. However, if it's already possible to live a unique experience as a spectator, imagine what is possible do for a player of an interactive story. And this is good time; imagination, that's your trade.

David, what have you learned about your players by the way they play?

David Cage: In *Detroit*, we implemented what we call telemetry. It's a technology that allows us to track what our players are doing in the game virtually in real time. We can see how much time they spend playing, where they get stuck, where they fail and, of course, the choices they make.

It's a fascinating tool in terms of sociology more than in terms of gameplay. We can see the part of the world where the players tend to have more empathy or how they react to oral dilemmas depending on their culture.

For example, we discovered that the players who most often choose options based on empathy are the Japanese. In Japan, close to 80% of the choices made were the most empathetic choices.

We also included more explicit questions in the main menu using an android name Chloé in the form of a questionnaire.

By chance do you have any anecdotes to tell about the players' reactions to your stories?

What's the biggest reward for an author, regardless of the medium? It's having people tell you that your work influenced their life, in one way or another. I have so many anecdotes that it would be impossible to tell them all, but one that comes immediately to mind is a player who wrote me a letter a few yeas ago about my game *Fahrenheit*.

In his letter, he told me that he was on the verge of killing himself and he went by a videogame store as he was getting ready to put an end to his days. By chance, he saw the box for *Fahrenheit*, which explained that it was possible to commit suicide in the game if your character got too depressed. That caught his attention, and he bought the game, went home and finished it in one go. The experienced offered by the game save his life because, after he was done, he didn't feel like killing himself anymore. This may seem crazy when your job is just to write video games, and then someone tells you that you saved someone's life, but this the kind of surprise can get.

We often receive very touching feedback from fans who write us. There was one in particular, a person who wrote us about *Beyond: Two Souls*. She told us that someone close to her was very sick, on the verge of dying, and that she was really having a hard time facing this reality. She said that playing *Beyond: Two Souls* helped her accept the situation. This is incredibly deep and serious, and I might be inclined to not believe it at first, but the fact is that we constantly get stories like this.

I have hundreds of similar anecdotes, and it's truly the best reward an author can receive: to be part of the lives of the people playing the games you write.

MINI-GAMES: 100% OBJECTIVE

Open worlds invite you to explore, and mini-games are an opportunity to add an extra layer to your universe. These come in a variety of forms (from day-to-day activities to the wildest, most unlikely ideas) and make your story part of a rich, coherent system. Aside from a few marginal players who are going do things 100%, these games give the impression that the smallest details have been thought out. Mini-games are an opportunity for the player to prolong her experience by strolling about in search of hidden items.

Watch Dogs offered a wide array of mini-games that really give it a certain flavor. On the other hand, *Final Fantasy* offers gameplay that includes cards games: notice to collectors.

ILLUSION AND PANACHE

There is a little magic behind all this, and we already talked about the illusion of choice, for example. You player anticipates, plays and imagines what's going to happen. So, you need to throw her off and steer her at the same time. She's going to have illusions, believe in the illusions you put forth, and, inevitably, they will go up in smoke.

Naturally, though, it's not about disillusioning the player by luring her with a sensational story and leave her with something that one wouldn't dare call an adventure.

As a magician of writing, you have to show you have panache: the player knows you're going to dupe her, just we know a magician does a trick. You announce the color, the player might well know what's going to happen, yet she's amazed by what she sizes.

A player won't begrudge you if you arouse her imagination and take beyond her what she was expecting. As opposed to a magic show, your story remains a game, however, so it's normal for the player to guess right and anticipate certain things. That's part of the joy of playing.

It's up to you to place your illusions in the right spots. Either the player is thrilled because the illusion reveals something even more crazy, or she's thrilled because behind this illusion she sees all the pieces of the machinery, like when she finally understands the big villain's plan, for example. Illusion and suspense will be connected on your end, and with your panache as an author, you will offer her a spectacle where she'll be a spectator, assistant and, lastly, a magician.

PROMISES AND REWARDS

In an interactive story, the notion of playing is essential, and your player is, thus, going to be rewarded. But does this mean that she wins then?

In a game where you break bricks to infinity and establish a score, the notion of victory is rather diluted, it's more of a performance we would say. If your game consists of rescuing hostages, then, yes, this is a victory if you succeed.

In interactive storytelling, the victory is the experience that player lives: the ending may be tragic, to put it another the player can lose, but if the adventure has kept its promises, the player will have had a beautiful gaming experience.

It is important to have ambition for a beautiful story to propose challenges that reward the player with an ending that meets, or exceeds, her expectations.

In an interactive game, the main character and the player are connected, so you can stimulate one or the other to seek adventure with a reward system. This can be as basic as money, allies, or apple trees. This depends on your story, but there needs to be a notion of progress, legitimate progress: it is announced that a given action will lead to a reward. You can have a go and throw the player off balance when it's your turn. Everything depends on the tone of your story.

Conversely, if the story is decline of the character, perhaps because the player has taken this path, successive losses despite great efforts will a certain dramatic effect. Until the very end the play will want to know whether she can do it.

Make big promises and give an even greater reward with a beautiful adventure. But don't forget that, in a game, you need to give rewards regularly. The main character's and the player's motivation may not be enough, and in a game, even if you regularly lose in a difficult story, some gains, even temporary ones, are expected. And these gains won't have much influence at all compared to all time the player has so happily spent in your story.

CONTROLLING THE MORAL STAKES

You need to show proof of illusion and prestige, you need to promise and reward, and a good way to make sure that you get all of this are moral stakes.

You have often read it in the chapters regarding the characters, their motivations will often be decisive in their moral choices, or in the dilemmas that you can offer them. And the player can also sometimes face a dilemma: *Should I do what my main character would normally do, or do I do something different?*

If you're writing an interactive narrative, it's not just to propose entering through a door or a window, to grab an ax or a pistol, to sell apples or lettuce.

The player has to calculate and anticipate the consequences of her choices as best as she can, based on the information she has at a given time. And what's going to help her decide is the notion of gaining or losing for her character. This isn't about physical, financial, etc. gain or loss, it's a moral gain or loss: in what direction is she evolving? How does the adventure transform the character, or how does the adventure reveal it.

In the game, if you start off as a manager in the produce department of a supermarket, and, at the end of the adventure, the person goes back to work, he will no longer be the same person. The family

This is a moral concern that often weighs on human beings, even if they haven't met their family. Because we aren't made in artificial wombs and ordered online, then educated in cocoons by artificial intelligence, family is fundamental. Thus, family relationships are fundamental. And pushing away, betraying, supporting and helping your family has serious consequences, whether the character's acts are legitimate, justified or not.

That said, not all games rely on genetic families, far from it. You need to this notion to close relations.

Close relations

The saying goes, you don't choose your parents, you choose your friends, the people you love, etc. You may even have a notion of extended family (with a tribe, a group of friends, brothers in arms, etc.), adoptive family, etc. Human beings have a herd instinct whether by obligation (family, birth place) or by choice (connections, friendships, etc.). As with family, behavior and moral choices regarding close relations have serious consequences.

Social status

What social status does the character have and what moral stakes are tied to it? For this social status also generates an expectation with respect to others. Morally, we expect greater things from a queen vampire, even if things get bloody, than from a Nerf salesman, even if he's perhaps traveled to the four corners of the earth. Moral stakes tied to social status are those for which the character is most likely to lie, betray, etc.

The self

And yes, after all these layers (family, close relations, society), to what extent does your character know himself and defines himself? Many games have an initiatory aspect even without saying so because, often, the character discovers his abilities and powers gradually, since, frequently, the player is learning at the same time. And in interactive storywriting, it is important to give the player real leeway to define the attitude of her character, and the consequences of her acts. Naturally, at first players are going to play as they see themselves in this universe, as they are portrayed, and not many of them are going to play differently right off the bat, make their way differently, unless it is made crystal clear from the moment they buy the game.

What's interesting with the advent of online games is studying the choices most often made by the players and seeing if there are significant trends. The explanation can be cultural, based on the story (this is the best choice to win), social, etc.

INVOLVING THE PLAYER BY ANY MEANS POSSIBLE

The three elements of involvement

1. Emotion	2. Ambition	3. Physical
Narrative	Career	Scene anticipation
Revelation	Recognition	HUD
Web of characters	Satisfaction	Combo
Empathy	Reputation	Mini-games

Avatar   Player

It's better to write so it's nice and legible, and we can't repeat it enough: involve the player. Whether it's through the characters, the action or the universe, involve the player, think of this every time you work on a scene. Don't make a scene just to create a connection in your arborescence; the player must really have something to do, and not just stack cubes.

Use your illusion, evince prestige, entice her, make her made, frustrate her, make her laugh and cry. Your story is a challenge, an adventure, your story becomes her story.

CONCLUSION 10 TIPS FOR WRITING AN INTERACTIVE STORY

As you can well imagine, we'll be concise. You need to be to fit everything we've touched on in 10 key points:

- Write the endings first, so that they are all interesting!
- Build a universe and respect its codes.
- Manage your time, stick to your deadline.
- Emotionally involve the player through your main character.
- Raise the stakes of the player's quest as high as you can!
- Each choice is a dilemma!
- The consequences must be felt in the short, medium and long term.
- The player must have witnesses to her actions.
- Frustrate and reward the player.
- Have your game tested, again and again!

It is now the dawn of the most extraordinary interactive adventure ever: your adventure!

We only have one more thing to tell you dear interactive author: write your stories and seize the incredible power of making everyone of us your hero!

Pierre Lacombe, Gabriel Féraud, Clément Rivière

AFTERWORD*: BRINGING YOUR INTERACTIVE STORY TO LIFE

When I arrived at Telltale, we tried to enhance our interactive scriptwriting skills even more. What we were trying to do, and what other studios are trying to do right now, is not stop the story, to make things move, to let you make decisions organically through this experience.

The true power comes when I can changes things profoundly, when I can make very powerful calculations to imagine how the story continues, when I can change the values in a big simulation with my behavior and have the simulation then evolve in a suitable type of narrative.

When we were working on Batman Season 2 at Telltale, we started experimenting with the timing and the sequence of the events... Such as the way you've treated John Doe throughout the episodes. How did John feel connected to you as friend? By putting trust in you? How far does he trust you? What was his connection with Harley? Making these connections among the many characters, and then having the final result be determined not just by one or two actions but the total number of combined actions as a whole, is what allows you to induce John to become the Joker in a different way. It's difficult to give the players the impression that they were going to determine what the Joker would become.

....

*From exclusive interviews.

It's very easy to begin a story, but it's hard to finish one. Begin at the ending, do it right. So, the first thing to explain is your vision of the player's experience. "Here's what we're trying to say this season, here are the emotions the player is going to live." So, in Batman Season 2, we knew that it was a matter of shaping the Joker. We want you to create the Joker that you want. How did we do this? We had directed the first episode with a team consisting of a lead writer, an animator and art director. This same team worked on episodes 1, 3, and 5, and a different team did 2 and 4. We had to work at the same time to make the 5 episodes during our time window. The bible of the season and production were managed by the season leads. We had two of them (one for episodes 1, 3 and 5, another for 2 and 4) as well as episodic leads. But in practice, sometimes there were complications. For example: "Whoa, we changed the scene" and suddenly, we had to rewrite a whole section after this scene. The original methodology had been to "be ready to rewrite episodes 2, 3, 4, 5, based on the audience's reactions to episode 1." So, perhaps we had already written episodes 2, 3, 4 and 5 and when we received feedback on the 1st episode, episode 2 was too far along to really change it, but 3 can change, 4 can change a lot, 5 can be totally rewritten. So, we were constantly reorganizing.

We did 18 episodes in 1 year. That's more than crazy. That required 4 teams, one per franchise and season. But 18 episodes was more than our audience was willing to consume, even our biggest fans. We saturated the market with our own products.

If you have an experienced team and you keep it together without breaking it up, try to have a creative vision planned out and defined as much as possible with a creative director who can map out the season's production. We had six weeks to write the season's arc and go into detail for each episode. But we never had enough time. We knew that the release on D-day, we had to finish the writing X days ahead of time, and that gave us the allotted time for writing. I think if you want to create a very profound narrative-based game, you have to give yourself a significant amount of time to map out the season, create strong characters with strong relationships, because that's what people will remember.

What's more, we were able to monitor which characters resonated with the players. We could literally see which decisions they would make, whether 95% of players would only see 5% of our content. This kind of thing can also be problem, if you spend a lot of time building a branch and no one plays it.

In practice, the team was very good at creating appealing content for each branch. When the players were on the whole voluntarily steered in their choices, we created twists to surprise them and divide them up again.

To let the people play with the web of characters and to manipulate their emotions, like in a soap opera. These are human relationships. Take great literature, imagine you can monitor the public's reaction in real time. This would be a very interesting database giving a snapshot of humanity. This is what we can do with our art form. You can basically ask the player what he feels, without being intrusive.

We make assumptions about what we see in public, but most people publicly reveal their best face. When you are alone, at home, relaxing and playing, you say different things about yourself.

For a society, it would be very interesting to know what people feel when they don't have their guard up. We would surely discover that, as humans, we have a lot of things in common, very positive things. But also very disturbing things for a small percentage. This is basically what we discovered.

We started to do data profiling at Telltale to give different types of feedback to players and show them their connection to the other players. It's a most interesting thing. You can compare yourself: for example, 85% of players made this choice, I would never have made this choice. These emotional profiles were created based on how the people played the game.

In 20 years, game technology will no longer be a production problem, just like the camera no longer is for audiovisual since it is very easy to use. The issue is more your look. Once narrative-based production tools can be accessed by everyone, everything will be played back on the story, which will become queen. Strong characters and big emotions are what people remember. Take season 1 of Telltale for example. It is still very powerful.

Save yourself time by basing things on an existing engine to quickly come to a result that allows you to tell a beautiful story that touches people, a story they'll talk about. This is where you will create your audience. You can then do a second part, and your audience will get even bigger. Take the Wizard of Oz, it's been such a huge cultural legacy for such a long time. What game will achieve this kind of enduring fame? Game remakes contribute to this sustainability by updating the technical expectations of the old games.

One day, someone will make a game that will touch the whole world for generations with the help of remakes and portability on several platforms. Our game Minecraft, for example, is available on Netflix, and you can play it on any device instantly. This is an incredible way to touch such a larger audience. The power to change things, to break someone's heart, to save someone, these kinds of interactions are very powerful.

When people are passionate about the characters we've created as if they are real, it's magical. I've followed Clémentine in his adventures. Tens of thousands of people still talk of "their Clémentine." I was so fortunate to be able to contribute to his adventure. In 10 years, I'm certain that if one thing must live on from my games, it will be Clémentine. This is a gift from the players to us.

Play the narrative-based games from all of the studios, analyze the codes of the genre, sometimes they're superficial, but it's up to you to decide. Ask yourself how you can empower your player so he can feel recognized. Invent new ways of achieving it. Take inspiration from elements of other games. Games in the horror genre are very good. They can frighten you and make you angry. How can I make people cry? Make them generous, make them fall in love? How do I allow them to feel strong positive emotions? You can go even further than us. Study psychology, behavioral analysis.

Write constantly. Use the simplest interactive scriptwriting tools to experiment. Once you have a touching story, think that you will need a team if you want ambitious staging. We had more than 100 people involved on each episode. But you can totally take a much more simple approach to staging. This is also the best setting for making mistakes. Start small.

The video game industry is going to continue to grow and become very strong. Now is the perfect time to join it by creating a multi-platform narrative-based game. All the big tech companies want this type of content. It's an incredible business opportunity. Get started and earn a lot of money!

David Bowman
Vice-President of Production (Telltale Games)

You've reached the end of this book. You have been the reader of this book, now it's time you fully assume your role as an author.

As you can imagine, more than anything an interactive story is where your spectator becomes active; he becomes the player and makes choices he wants to experience the consequences of. You must accept the fact that he is the director and co-producer of the story. Few media allow this: there is interactive cinema and theater, some video games and, of course, roleplaying games.

You no longer fully control your narrative. You must agree to sacrifice a potentially better story. Indeed, in a linear script, you might have chosen the best of all the possible combinations to write the best story, and the best ending. In an interactive script, the author writes several types of possible combinations, which will be more or less interesting. And the player is the one who writes "his story" by making his choices. In this way, the interactive scriptwriter offers the players empathy and involvement.

In general, an interactive work means sacrificing your desire for the perfect story in order to involve the player in the work you're offering.

You need to train yourself how to write interactive stories. First, for yourself. When I was 19, I started a roleplaying game club where I was would write a story a week, which was a crazy amount of work but very educational.

Next, for everyone else. When I started writing roleplaying game stories not just for myself anymore, but for others, I had to write full stories that other people had to be able to read and understand without my help, which was a real challenge. You'll quickly see what works and what doesn't.

That is, in a professional environment. So, you'll definitely gather a lot of documentation here. You'll learn the codes, and, here, this is a valuable lesson, often because you won't agree with the aim (or even on the subject you're writing about). But acquiring the methods will help you pace your story.

This experience and these new skills are going to allow you to interactive stories differently. When *Heavy Rain* came out, I took it as an interactive film and found it fascinating. It's virtually one of a kind in the videogame world. Up until then, I thought that only roleplaying games could offer so many branches. This new vision changed my life, and I embraced my new destiny.

Ten years later, my determination has paid off. I work at Quantic Dream, one of the three big cinematographic videogame schools, which does interactive stories with the codes of cinema. There is also Kojima, which attempts to do cinema and which, ultimately, does video games. Lastly, there's Naughty Dogs, which is situated in the middle. There are some no less magnificent games such as *The Last of Us*, which are video games that mine the codes of cinema to further blur the lines between the two mediums. None of these three schools is better than the others. It's up to your to decide your fate, the future of interactive storytelling.

Because admit it, the specter of triple A productions (very big productions) has been reduced to nothing. While studios such as Dontnod are marvelous exceptions, the future of this one-of-a-kind format is especially in demand at independent studios. The more propositions there are, the more the quality and the ideas will respond to either other. Video games are like cinema, they're constantly evolving and advancing the state of the art.

And last piece of advice, making roleplaying games by taking inspiration from all of your entertainment experiences. Immerse yourself with keeping count. You need to read a lot to open up and see what things are done best in all the arts (theater, film, etc.) because that's going to involve new reflection on you part, and new results. It's a good thing to use ideas from other media in interactive storytelling because that leads to reconstructions, solving, along the way, many of your problems.

I hope this book allows you to open up and have confidence in yourself. Writing a classic story is already complicated, so know that your interest in interactive stories gives you head start. But the adventure is far from over, many choices and dilemmas await you. So, never forget, no matter the situation, it's up to you to play!

Benjamin Diebling
Shooting director in *Detroit : Become Human*, roleplaying game author

INDEX

reward, 217

rewrite, 30

roleplaying game, 37, 76, 81, 151, 156, 202

roleplaying, 37, 74

rough sketch, 179

RPG, 37, 40

S

"sandbox" scenario, 38

save, 178, 199

science fiction, 76, 97

script, 46

secondary character, 116, 128, 130, 140, 145, 199, 210

secondary ending, 28, 185

secondary mission, 128

sequence, 42

serious game, 35

skill choices, 191

social status, 219

specifications, 212

spectator, 140, 142

spell check, 174, 175

sports game, 24

statement of intent, 66

step outline, 65

story, 27

story you play, 23

strategy, 28, 32

strip, 51

structure based on the spring, 89

subjective camera, 137

supporting actor, 126

suspense, 156

switch, 102

synopsis, 66

syntax, 174

T

telemetry, 215

text-based game, 83, 84

time management, 61

time, 60, 215, 217

tragedy, 89

trigger event, 119, 133, 136, 138

trigger incident, 135

triple A, 86

Twine, 85, 179

twist, 98, 101

U

universe, 36, 97, 108, 115, 128

unusual languages, 145

V

variables, 181

video game, 19, 45, 109, 144, 152, 158, 161, 203

visual novel, 156

W

wargame(s), 73, 109

whodunit, 184

witness, 128, 129

working in stages, 90

world expansion, 110

World of Warcraft, 25

world's end, 110

Thank you for choosing this Eyrolles book. We hope you found this read interesting and inspiring.

We would be thrilled to stay in contact with you and be able to offer you other ideas about books to discover, new arrivals, tips, events with our authors and game contests.

Interested? Sign up for our newsletter.

To do so, go to go.eyrolles.com/newsletter or scan this QR code (your email address will be used solely by Eyrolles to send you the requested information):

Thank you for trusting in us.

The Eyrolles team

P.S.: five readers are selected at random from new newsletter subscribers each month to each win three books of their choice from the Eyrolles catalog. To enter the drawing, just sign up at go.eyrolles.com/newsletter (game rules available on the site)

Legal notice: January 2019
Printed in Poland by Interak